UNEP

Labour and the Environment: A Natural Synergy

UNEP Job Number: DPD/0856/NA

Disclaimers

Reproduction

Produced by

Major Groups and Stakeholders Branch (MGSB)
Division of Regional Cooperation (DRC)
United Nations Environment Programme

P. O. Box. 30552 Nairobi, Kenya
Tel. +(254) 20 762 43 30
Fax. +(254) 20 762 50 10

Email: civil.society@unep.org
Website: http://www.unep.org/civil_society/

Printing

Printed in Malta by Progress Press Co. Ltd

Distribution

SMI Distribution Services, Ltd, UK

This publication is available from Earthprint.com (http://www.earthprint.com)

Illustrations

On the occasion of the Trade Union Assembly on Labour and the Environment / WILL 2006 in January 2006, UNEP compiled a dossier of photographs from its own collection of images. These photographs were presented in an exhibition called "Labour and the Environment", which ran concurrently with the meeting. They illustrated the close linkages between the world of work and the environment. They also showed how employees at the lowest end of the wage scale do the dirtiest jobs, have the least job security and are too often the most vulnerable to environmental risks.

The photographs in this publication come from that exhibition.

Acknowledgements

UNEP acknowledges the contributions made by many individuals and institutions to the preparation and publication of Labour and the Environment: A Natural Synergy. The Production Team and list of authors are listed below. Special thanks are also extended to colleagues from the International Labour Organization (ILO), the World Health Organization (WHO), the International Trade Union Confederation (ITUC), and its member organisations as well as the International Labour Foundation for Sustainable Development (Sustainlabour).

Production Team

Coordinator

❏ Fatou NDOYE, Programme Officer, Major Groups and Stakeholders Branch, Division of Regional Cooperation, United Nations Environment Programme

Editor

❏ John SMITH, Consultant / Editor Environmental Publications

Reviewers

❏ Kilaparti RAMAKRISHNA, Policy Advisor, Office of the Executive Director, United Nations Environment Programme
❏ Nick NUTTALL, Spokesperson, Office of the Executive Director, United Nations Environment Programme

Cover Design

❏ United Nations Office at Nairobi, Publishing Services Section (UNON)

Graphics and Page Layout

❏ United Nations Office at Nairobi, Publishing Services Section (UNON)

List of Authors

Authors are listed in alphabetical order:

- ❏ Gerd Albracht, Senior Specialist, Occupational Safety and Health and Coordinator, Development of Inspection Systems, International Labour Organization
- ❏ Nilvo Luis Alves Da Silva, Officer in Charge, Major Groups and Stakeholders Branch, Division of Regional Cooperation, United Nations Environment Programme
- ❏ Sophie De Coninck, Programme Officer, Major Groups and Stakeholders Branch, Division of Regional Cooperation, United Nations Environment Programme
- ❏ Igor Fedotov, Senior Specialist, International Programme for Safety and Health at Work and the Environment (SafeWork), International Labour Organization
- ❏ Hilary French, Special Advisor, Major Groups and Stakeholders Branch, Division of Regional Cooperation, United Nations Environment Programme and Senior Advisor for Programs, Worldwatch Institute
- ❏ Ivan D. Ivanov, Occupational Health Programme (SDE/PHE), World Health Organization
- ❏ Corey Kaplan, Development of Inspection Systems, SafeWork, International Labour Organization
- ❏ Olfa Khazri, Sustainable Development Group, Policy Integration Department, International Labour Organization
- ❏ Tony Musu, Research Officer, Health and Safety Department, European Trade Union Institute for Research, Education and Health and Safety (ETUI-REHS), European Trade Union Confederation (ETUC)
- ❏ Fatou Ndoye, Programme officer, Major Groups and Stakeholders Branch, Division of Regional Cooperation, United Nations Environment Programme
- ❏ Joaquín Nieto, President, Sustainlabour Foundation
- ❏ Lene Olsen, Bureau for Workers' Activities, International Labour Organization
- ❏ Peter PoSchen, Sustainable Development Group, Policy Integration Department, International Labour Organization
- ❏ Lucien Royer, Occupational Health Safety Environment and Sustainable Development Director, Trade Union Advisory Committee to the OECD (TUAC), International Trade Union Confederation (ITUC)
- ❏ Shizue Tomoda, Senior Sectoral Specialist, Sectoral Activities (SECTOR), International Labour Organization
- ❏ Cornis Van der Lugt, Corporate Social Responsibility (CSR) Programme Officer, Division of Technology, Industry and Economics, United Nations Environment Programme
- ❏ Monika Wehrle-MacDevette, Programme Officer, Division of Regional Cooperation, United Nations Environment Programme
- ❏ Adriana Zacarias Farah, Project Co-ordinator, Division of Technology, Industry and Economics, United Nations Environment Programme
- ❏ Daniela Zampini, Multinational Enterprises Programme, International Labour Organization

Table of Contents

Foreword

abour and the Environment: A Natural Synergy was born out of the Trade Union Assembly on Labour and the Environment, which was also called WILL 2006, held at UNEP's headquarters in Nairobi, Kenya, on 15-17 January 2006.

The Assembly, organized in cooperation with the International Labour Organization (ILO) and the World Health Organization (WHO), was part of UNEP's continuing efforts to enhance participation by major groups in international environmental processes.

The Assembly was not the first occasion on which UNEP had collaborated with ILO, or with workers and trade unions. Almost ten years earlier, UNEP entered into a Memorandum of Understanding with ILO to work in four main areas of mutual interest: the working environment; human settlements; environment and development; and education and training. Moreover, during the World Summit on Sustainable Development (WSSD) in Johannesburg in 2002, a conference on "Fashioning a New Deal" was jointly organized by UNEP, ILO, the International Confederation of Free Trade Unions (ICFTU) and the Trade Union Advisory Committee (TUAC) to the Organization for Economic Cooperation and Development (OECD). "Fashioning a New Deal" was a global call to place humans at the centre of development, and to include a social justice dimension in sustainable development policies.

The Assembly solidified and advanced these core values. All partners were able to renew their commitments and to agree on a common agenda for future action. Indeed, the meeting's Final Resolution constitutes a commitment – by all partners – to promote more integrated approaches to the design and implementation of sustainable development policies, incorporating labour, public health and environmental issues.

The resounding conclusion of the Assembly was that we have decisively moved into a new era – and that the perception or myth that environment is somehow at odds with jobs and economic development is outdated.

Workers and their trade unions can make a significant and positive difference to the sustainable management of the environment and ecosystems. Workers are social agents directly associated with the production chain. Meanwhile, workers are all too often among the first victims of environmental damage.

This publication, entitled Labour and the Environment: A Natural Synergy, presents examples of the application of technical expertise, of workplace participation, and of tools that promote workers' health and safety to problems that extend beyond the workplace into areas such as environmental protection, public health and the accountability of employers.

It focuses on crucial issues ranging from climate change and energy, chemicals management, and corporate social responsibility and accountability to future involvement of workers and trade unions with the environment and with efforts to move towards sustainability.

In addition, examples are cited of the incorporation of environmental matters in collective bargaining and in agreements at the workplace, nationally and internationally.

UNEP, ILO and WHO are committed to maintaining and improving their cooperation, so as to further integrate their approaches to labour, environment and public health.

UNEP has recently begun a project to support concrete initiatives aimed at environmental protection and increased trade union capacity for participation in environmental policy-making at the international level.

Labour and the Environment: A Natural Synergy is the result of cooperation between UNEP, ILO and WHO, as well as workers and trade unions – the latter represented by the International Trade Union Confederation (ITUC) and the International Labour Foundation for Sustainable Development (Sustainlabour). I hope this publication will contribute to a better understanding of the links between labour and the environment, and to shaping social and environmental policies for sustainable development.

Achim Steiner

United Nations Under-Secretary General and
Executive Director of the United Nations Environment Programme

Introduction

Fatou Ndoye, *Major Groups and Stakeholders Branch, Division of Regional Cooperation, United Nations Environment Programme*

L abour and the Environment has long been perceived as an issue vested with highly conflicting interests. Most of the world population relies on natural resources and the environment for wages, if not simply for survival. Many workers share the fear that strengthened environmental policies will lead to job losses. However, perceptions of conflicting interests have evolved over the years. A number of studies, as well as practical experience, have made it clear that changing production and consumption patterns and adopting new techniques and methods – which are among the alternative ways out of the current environmental crisis – will foster job creation. Protecting our natural resource base and the environment will actually contribute to protecting employment and fighting poverty.

As an example, in 2004 there were more than 4.5 million "green power" consumers in Europe, the United States, Canada, Australia and Japan. These consumers purchased power voluntarily at the retail level or used "renewable energy certificates".[1] Direct jobs worldwide from renewable energy manufacturing, operations and maintenance exceeded 1.7 million in the same year, including some 0.9 million jobs related to biofuels production (REN21 2005). Between 2004 and 2005, investment in the renewable energy sector worldwide grew from US$30 billion to US$38 billion; biomass power production grew by 50-100 per cent in several countries; biodiesel production grew by 85 per cent (with nine EU countries becoming producers for the first time); grid-tied solar power grew by 55 per cent (led by Germany, which now has more than 200 000 solar rooftops); and solar hot water capacity grew by 23 per cent in China as well as reaching record levels in Europe (REN21 2006).[2]

These figures demonstrate that moving towards sustainability and creating more jobs are compatible goals. In this context, it is crucial that linkages between Labour and the Environment are adequately addressed in order to build a new economic model – based on global participation, social equity and equality – which will also be environmentally sound and sustainable. Only then will we be able to meet the challenges underlined by the Millennium Development Goals adopted in 2000,[3] reach the targets agreed at the

---

1   Energy certificates: Tradable renewable energy certificates represent "the certified generation of one unit of renewable energy (typically one MWh). These certificates allow trading or renewable energy obligations among consumers and/or producers, and in some markets like the United States allow anyone to purchase separately the green power 'attributes' of renewable energy." Utility green pricing occurs when "a utility offers its customers a choice of power products, usually at differing prices, offering varying degrees of renewable energy content. The utility guarantees to generate or purchase enough renewable energy to meet the needs of all green power customers." (Definitions from the REN21 Renewable Energy Policy Network (www.ren21.net). The United States Department of Energy's "Energy and Energy Efficiency" web page provides this definition of certificates: "Renewable energy certificates (RECs), also known as green certificates, green tags, or tradable renewable certificates, represent the environmental attributes of the power produced from renewable energy projects and are sold separately from commodity electricity. Customers can buy green certificates whether or not they have access to green power through their local utility or a competitive electricity marketer. And they can purchase green certificates without having to switch electricity suppliers" www.eere.energy.gov/greenpower/markets/certificates.shtml?page=0).

2   The Renewables 2005 Global Status Report, 2006 Update, www.ren21.net. See, in particular, Chapter 3, section 1, "Climate change and energy" by Peter Poschen and Olfa Khazri.

3   The eight Millennium Development Goals (MDGs) were adopted at the UN Millennium Summit in September 2000. The MDGs are time-bound, measurable goals and targets for combating poverty, hunger, disease, illiteracy, environmental degradation, and discrimination against women. The Summit's Millennium Declaration also outlined a wide range of commitments on human rights, good governance and democracy (www.un.org/millenniumgoals/).

World Summit on Sustainable Development in Johannesburg in 2002[4] and restore human dignity.

Increasing pressures on the environment

The human population is expected to reach 6.4 billion in 2005. Estimates are that it will top 8.1 billion in 2030, and that there will be between 8.7 and 11.3 billion people on the earth in 2050 (UNEP 2002 and 2005, WRI 2005).

Consumption of both goods and services provide opportunities for a healthy and satisfying life, including employment, mobility, education and adequate nutrition. However, among the factors leading to natural resource depletion and pressures on ecosystems, consumption has had the greatest impact and caused the most direct harm. Much harm has resulted from the overconsumption of animals and plants, mining of soil nutrients, and other forms of biological depletion. Ecosystems have also suffered considerable indirect harm from pollution and wastes originating in agriculture, industry and energy production. Pollution and wastes are, of course, associated with unsustainable patterns and levels of consumption.

Pressures on natural resources and the environment – and their unsustainable exploitation – are expected to continue to increase dramatically, despite the efforts made to reverse these trends over a period of more than 30 years. A casual glance at *One Planet Many People: Atlas of Our Changing Environment* (UNEP 2005) reveals that since the beginning of the 20th century:

- ❑ Logging and land use conversion have reduced forest cover by at least 20 per cent, and possibly as much as 50 per cent;
- ❑ Nearly 70 per cent of the world's major marine fish stocks have been overfished or are being fished at the biological limit;
- ❑ Dams and other engineering works have fragmented 60 per cent of the world's large river systems, and have so impeded water flow that the time it takes for a drop of water to reach the sea has tripled;
- ❑ Human activities are significantly altering the basic chemical cycles upon which all ecosystems depend.

The current global economic pattern has exacerbated existing environmental pressures. Globalization, which is imposing new dynamics on socio-economic development, is of basic importance with respect to the crucial issue of economic development vs. environment and (sustainable) development. Over roughly the past 30 years the environment has been subjected to stresses resulting from an 18-fold increase in world economic output (UNEP 2002).

Engaging civil society and stakeholders in the work of UNEP

UNEP's mandate is to co-ordinate the development of environmental policy consensus by keeping the global environment under review and bringing emerging issues to the attention of governments and the international community for action. Its activities have increasingly focused on environment for development, highlighting the central role in human well-being of ecosystems and the services they provide.

---

4   The Johannesburg Plan of Implementation was agreed in 2002 at the conclusion of the World Summit on Sustainable Development (WSSD) (www.un.org/esa/sustdev/documents/WSSD_POI_PD/English/POIToc.htm).

Since its inception, UNEP has enjoyed a special relationship with civil society in tackling environmental issues. In 2002 UNEP's Executive Director was requested "to further develop, and review and revise as necessary the strategy for engaging civil society in the programme of activities of the United Nations Environment Programme ... to ensure that all programmes take into account opportunities for multi-stakeholder participation in design, implementation, monitoring of activities, and dissemination of outputs."[5]

To this end, UNEP has hosted a number of noteworthy events to strengthen participation and consultation with major groups, including the annual Global Civil Society Forum (GCSF)[6] and the Global Women's Assembly on Environment – Women As the Voice for the Environment (WAVE).[7]

Workers and trade unions are among the largest and most important major groups of civil society,[8] with increasing interaction with UNEP's activities and policy dialogue since 2002. According to Chapter 29 of Agenda 21, "workers and trade unions should play an active role in the sustainable development activities of international and regional organizations, particularly within the United Nations system."[9] UNEP's current initiative to build a partnership on labour and the environment is an extension of its efforts to engage *major groups and stakeholders* in its work and to establish a meaningful dialogue with civil society, as key stakeholders in the international environmental policy arena. [10]

The objectives of the initiative were:

(i)   to reinforce the social and labour dimension of environmental conservation and sustainable development,

(ii)   to strengthen the relationship between UNEP and the world of labour in addressing the integration of an equitable industrial development and environmental protection,

(iii)   to address the gap in representation of workers and trade unions in international environmental processes, as they can uniquely stimulate debate around the social

---

5   Decision SS.VII/5 of the Seventh Special Session of the Governing Council/Global Ministerial Environment Forum (GC/GMEF) of UNEP of 15th February.

6   The Global Civil Society Forum (GCSF) is held in conjunction with the UNEP Governing Council/Global Ministerial Environment Forum (www.unep.org/civil_society/GCSF/index.asp).

7   The first "Global Women's Assembly on Environment: Women as the Voice for the Environment" (WAVE) was held at UNEP headquarters in Nairobi on 11-13 October 2004. It was attended by some 150 participants from 65 countries (www.unep.org/civil_society/WAVE/default.asp).

8   Women; children and youth; indigenous people and their communities; non-governmental organizations (NGOs); local authorities; workers and trade unions; business and industry; the scientific and technological community farmers. See Agenda 21, Section III (www.un.org/esa/sustdev/mgroups/mgroups.htm).

9   Agenda 21 is one of five agreements adopted at the 1992 UN Conference on Environment and Development (UNCED) in Rio de Janeiro. "These [agreements] establish governing principles and commit governments to a range of post-Rio processes, centred upon the provision of national reports which may be compared internationally and against a limited set of goals established. Agenda 21 forms the general guiding document for pursuing sustainable development and initiates significant institutional changes" (Grubb and others, 1993, p. xiii). Chapter 29 of Agenda 21 focuses on strengthening the role of workers and their trade unions in sustainable development activities. "[Its] main concern is 'poverty alleviation and full and sustainable employment, which contribute to safe, clean and healthy environments...' Tripartite collaboration between governments, trade unions and employers' organizations should be established, particularly on the implementation of Agenda 21. ILO conventions on workers' freedom of association and on the right to organize should be ratified and implemented. Environmental policies should be jointly developed by workers' and employers' organizations. Workers and trade unions should have access to relevant information. Education, training and retraining programmes, particularly on the working environment, should be strengthened. Other trade union activities should focus on participation in sustainable development activities of local communities and on regional and international organizations" (Grubb and others, 1993, pp. 139-40). The complete text of Agenda 21 is available on the UN Division of Sustainable Development site (www.un.org/esa/sustdev/documents/agenda21).

10 See the UNEP Major Groups and Stakeholders Branch website (www.unep.org/civil_society/major_groups).

aspects of sustainable development while at the same time contributing to the debate on economic and environmental dimensions.

The process of engagement has been initiated in June 2005, in close consultation and collaboration with the workers and trade unions, in an attempt to build greater ownership of the engagement process into the trade union movement. This process has yielded, among other activities, the Trade Union Assembly on Labour and the Environment / WILL 2006 and this publication.

The Trade Union Assembly on Labour and the Environment / WILL 2006

The Trade Union Assembly on Labour and the Environment / WILL 2006 was attended by 180 participants from every part of the world with 120 delegates from trade union organizations and federations, representing over 200 million workers in more than 50 countries. Most of the world's largest trade union organizations participated. The participants considered the role of workers in promoting sustainable development. They discussed and made recommendations on a wide range of environmentally related labour issues, including:

❏ Global climate change and its implications for the world of work;
❏ Prevention of hazardous chemicals at the workplace;
❏ Occupational, public and environmental health;
❏ Trade unions' actions for equal and sustainable access to resources and services;
❏ Participation in environmental governance by trade unions and workers;
❏ Corporate social responsibility (CSR) and accountability.

One way participants shared their experiences and concerns was through the presentation of case studies focused on trade union involvement in the environmental agenda, and on workers' health and the workplace. Several of these case studies are included in *Labour and the Environment: A Natural Synergy*. They demonstrate a commitment by workers and trade unions to a more sustainable future; they also demonstrate that concrete changes, aiming at sustainable development, are already taking place.

A common framework for action and final recommendations were discussed during the meeting, as well as challenges in regard to implementation. The Final Resolution adopted at the conclusion of the meeting (Annex 1) highlights workers' commitment to integrating the environmental pillar of sustainable development.[11] The Final Resolution sets out a number of common objectives. It also expresses support for engaging further with UNEP, ILO and WHO in implementing the Resolution's various provisions and paving the way for Workers' Initiatives for a Lasting Legacy (WILL).

Workers and trade unions, and the UN partners involved in the meeting, agreed to assist in the *replication of successful case studies* presented during the meeting, and to work in other fields of mutual interest including *training and education on the latest developments in*

---

11 The three pillars of sustainable development are economic development, social development and environmental protection.

international environmental law in areas such as the newly adopted chemicals treaties (e.g. the Stockholm Convention on Persistent Organic Pollutants).[12]

Labour and the Environment: a publication building on the work accomplished

Labour and the Environment: a Natural Synergy builds on the outcome of the Trade Union Assembly on Labour and the Environment / WILL 2006. Its purpose is to stimulate continued reflection, and to highlight directions for future research and potential partnerships.

Labour and the Environment: A Natural Synergy is also intended to raise awareness of the inter-relationships among various sustainable development stakeholders, and to expand on the role that workers, in particular, can play in promoting sustainable development, especially with reference to its environmental pillar.

Labour and the Environment: A Natural Synergy is authored by contributors from the organizations partner to the UNEP initiative. It features perspectives from UNEP, ILO, WHO and from workers and trade unions on issues of participation into international environmental processes and participation of the trade union movement into the global debate on globalization.

A number of case studies were presented during the Trade Union Assembly on Labour and the Environment / WILL 2006. They will feature in this publication as examples and illustrations of the initiatives taken within the world of labour.

Chapter 1 reviews the natural synergy between labour and the environment. An outline is provided of linkages and of the complimentarity between the two. The value of protecting the environment is explored, along with impacts on employment and poverty reduction.

Chapter 2 considers relationships between UNEP, ILO, WHO, workers and trade unions and reaffirms the commitment made by workers and trade unions at the Trade Union Assembly on Labour and the Environment / WILL 2006 to make environment and sustainable development a priority and a focus of collective bargaining.

Chapter 3 provides the partners' positions on specific issues, such as climate change and energy; public access to services and commodities; occupational, environmental and public health; and chemical risks and hazardous substances and their inter-relations with and impacts on workers, the world of labour and trade unions.

Chapter 4 addresses perspectives for the future and a 'common framework for action'. This chapter, in particular, is a 'call to action' and contains messages on sustainable consumption and production patterns, corporate social responsibility and accountability, education, capacity building and knowledge sharing, interactions with other major groups and stakeholders, and how to foster the involvement of trade unions in the global and national environmental agendas.

---

12   The Stockholm Convention is a global treaty to protect human health and the environment from persistent organic pollutants (POPs). These chemicals remain intact in the environment for long periods, become widely distributed geographically, accumulate in the fatty tissue of living organisms, and are toxic to humans and wildlife (www.pops.int).

Labour and the Environment: A Natural Synergy addresses critical issues such as the importance of providing for just employment transitions. It reports on initiatives adopted throughout the world to reduce pressures on natural resources and the environment while leading to job creation. This publication will contribute to a common understanding of the nexus between labour, the environment and sustainable development, and of the need to build partnerships and alliances to forge an environmentally sustainable global economy.

References

- Grubb, M., M. Koch, A. Munson, F. Sullvian and K. Thomson (1993). *The Earth Summit Agreements: A Guide and Assessment. An Analysis of the Rio '92 UN Conference on Environment and Development.* Royal Institute of International Affairs and Earthscan, London.

- REN21 Renewable Energy Policy Network (2005). *Renewables: 2005 Global Status Report* (www.ren21.net).

— (2006) *Renewables: 2006 Global Status Report* (www.ren21.net).

- UNEP (2002). *Global Environment Outlook (GEO-3)* (www.unep.org/geo/geo3).

— (2003). Enhancing Civil Society Engagement in the Work of the United Nations Environment Programme: Strategy Paper (UNEP/GC.22/INF/13) (www.unep.org/civil_society/PDF_docs/Enhancing_Civil_Society_Engagement_In_UNEP.pdf).

— (2005) *One Planet, Many People: Atlas of our Changing Environment* (http://na.unep.net/OnePlanetManyPeople/index.php).

- WRI (World Resources Institute) (2005). *The Wealth of the Poor: Managing Ecosystems to Fight Poverty* (www.wri.org/biodiv/pubs_description.cfm?pid=4073).

Labour and the Environment: A Natural Synergy

1. Labour and the Environment: A Natural Synergy

Sophie De Coninck, *Major Groups and Stakeholders Branch, Division of Regional Cooperation, United Nations Environment Programme and* **Hilary French**, *Major Groups and Stakeholders Branch, Division of Regional Cooperation, United Nations Environment Programme and Senior Advisor for Programs, Worldwatch Institute*

© *Juan Pablo Ortiz / UNEP*

Deforestation, Columbia: *Rainforests are being destroyed because the value of the forested land is perceived as only the value of its timber by multi-national logging companies and land owners. More than 20 per cent of the world's oxygen is produced in the Amazon rainforest. When the timber is harvested for short-term gain and profit, the medicinal plants and other sustainable resources that thrive in the delicate ecosystem are destroyed.*

> *Creating decent and secure jobs is only possible… if environmental sustainability is attained…*
>
> Resolution of the Trade Union Assembly on Labour and the
> Environment / WILL 2006

Environmental protection, often perceived as a threat to economic development and jobs, is increasingly viewed by many people as a long-term tool to fight poverty and generate employment. However, many workers share the fear that strengthened environmental policies will lead to job losses. Any legitimate response to these concerns must answer the following questions:

- ❑ How can environmental and employment objectives be achieved and bring about new prospects?

- ❑ How can environmental issues be given proper attention by the world of labour in its efforts to face hunger, severe poverty or loss of jobs?

- ❑ How can environmental issues be relevant to workers?

Exploring the multiple linkages between labour and the environment can shed some light on these important questions.

The value of protecting the environment

The multidimensional value of the environment is increasingly acknowledged by economists and policy-makers around the world.

We all rely on ecosystems and the services they provide for food, water, energy and many other resources. Over the past 50 years humanity has altered ecosystems more rapidly and extensively than in any comparable period of its history. About 60 per cent of the world's ecosystem services, as assessed by the Millennium Ecosystem Assessment, are currently being degraded or used unsustainably – driven, among other factors, by increased economic activity, pollution, overexploitation and climate change (Millenium Ecosystem Assessment 2005).[13] According to the World Business Council for Sustainable Development, "Business cannot function if ecosystems and the services they deliver – like water, biodiversity, fibre, food and climate – are degraded or out of balance." [14] Although protecting ecosystems can pose threats to business and industry and create risks (e.g. related to increased costs or legal obligations), it can also generate new opportunities in many sectors, including agri-business, tourism, mining, forestry and energy.

In the face of rising energy prices and other threats (including, of course, climate change), new opportunities are emerging in areas such as renewable energy, energy efficiency, emissions trading and the transportation and construction sectors. The market for clean energy technologies could be worth US$1.9 trillion by 2020 (UNEP Finance Initiative 2002). These new growth areas contribute not only to climate change mitigation, but also

---

13   The Millennium Ecosystem Assessment (MA) is an international work programme designed to meet the needs of decision-makers and the public for scientific information about the consequences of ecosystem change for human well-being, and options for responding to those changes. Launched by UN Secretary-General Kofi Annan in 2001, it was completed in March 2005. The MA will help to meet the assessment needs of the Convention on Biological Diversity, the Convention to Combat Desertification, the Ramsar Convention on Wetlands and the Convention on Migratory Species, as well as the needs of other users in the private sector and civil society. If the MA proves useful to stakeholders, it is anticipated that such integrated assessments will be repeated every five to ten years and that ecosystem assessments will be regularly conducted on national or sub-national scales (www.maweb.org).

14   The World Business Council for Sustainable Development (WBCSD) is a non-profit organization bringing together some 180 international companies in a shared commitment to sustainable development through economic growth, ecological balance and social progress (www.wbcsd.ch).

to energy independence and job creation. They may eventually help to limit energy price fluctuations, which negatively impact the labour market. For each one percentage point reduction in the global GDP growth rate resulting from higher energy prices, the ILO estimates that net employment growth will be reduced by 9 to 10 million jobs worldwide (ILO 2006).

In addition, investors are increasingly interested in companies that implement industry-wide best practices aimed at working towards sustainability. Socially responsible investment worldwide was US$2 000 billion in 2004 (Fussler 2004). By going beyond basic legislative requirements, companies may expect competitive advantages derived, among others, from improved managerial performance and productivity, innovation, profitable environmentally related investments, reduced risks and greater consumer demand for sustainable products. Thus environmental, social and corporate responsibility can benefit companies and their workers. Protecting the environment generates economic returns which can then be channelled into other sustainable and profitable investments – creating a "virtuous circle".

On the other hand, failure to protect the environment could be hugely expensive. Although the overall cost of biodiversity loss is unknown, it can be partially estimated (including the costs of lost bioprospecting opportunities, lost carbon storage, lost tourism revenues and lost watershed protection). These very partial costs amount to tens of billions of dollars (Heal 2005). India alone loses more than US$10 billion annually (4.5 per cent of its GDP) due to environmental decline, with human induced land degradation responsible for productivity losses of around US$2.4 billion (UNEP 2002). This is a tremendous loss when one considers that a GDP growth rate of 5 to 6 per cent is required in South Asia to halve working poverty (ILO 2004-05).[15]

Globally, the frequency and cost of natural disasters – increasingly linked with environmental decline – are rising dramatically. The 2005 hurricane season may cost insurers as much as US$60 billion, more than double the amount in any previous year. Since the 1960s, according to Munich Re,[16] the economic cost of natural catastrophes has risen seven-fold and insured losses have risen 16-fold. The Association of British Insurers further reports that costs from windstorm-related damage will increase to an average US$27 billion per year by 2080 (UNEP Finance Initiative 2005).

In the absence of greatly stepped up policy response to climate change, the economic and social costs of the problem are likely to be staggering in coming decades, according to a groundbreaking recent study of the issue conducted by economist Sir Nicholas Stern on behalf of the UK Chancellor of the Exchequer. The Stern Review concluded that the economic and social disruptions caused by climate change could be "on a scale similar to

---

15 The working poor may be defined as those who work and who belong to poor households. Definition of the working poor involves two statistical units: individual and household. Individual is the basis for establishing the classification "working " or "not working" and household is the basis for establishing the classification "poor" or "not poor"; hence the category of those who are part of poor households but earn higher than poverty-line incomes (assuming that these are set) and those who earn less than poverty-line incomes but are part of non-poor households. Clearly household sizes, and the distribution of earners and dependents in households, can vary; furthermore, there are income transfers across households. The poor household is a result of all these factors. Estimation of the number of working poor at a country level takes such factors into consideration (ILO 2001, 2006).

16 The Munich Re Group is one of the world's largest reinsurers. It reinsures the risks of oil rigs, satellites and natural catastrophes, as well as those arising from genetic engineering, information technology, corporate management and many other activities (www.munichre.com).

those associated with the great wars and the economic depression of the first half of the 20th century" by later in the century and early in the next (Stern 2006).

Based on these figures, the choice might seem relatively easy. But harvesting the benefits of protecting the environment requires a long-term and a macro-level approach, while people's realities are different, shaped by their individual, shorter-term concerns.

In this context, recognizing the value of the environment does not mean denying the associated uncertainties and difficulties inherent in any major societal change, such as turbulence and changes in the labour market. Rather, it requires finding the way towards a *just transition*.

The impact of environmental protection on employment and poverty reduction: towards a just transition

Moving away from fossil fuel use, phasing out dangerous chemicals, and shifting to cleaner and more efficient technologies are major challenges for the global economy.

Although the evidence does not suggest that environmental protection measures are not a significant source of long-term job losses (Morgenstern and others 2002, Renner 2000, Wagner 2005), shifting to sustainable production and consumption patterns will require adjustments or significant changes in employment patterns in the short term. Efforts should therefore be made to integrate environmental policies and just employment transition measures, so that workers who are negatively affected by societal and economic changes are provided with educational and retraining programmes and decent employment alternatives (serving long-term community sustainability) or compensation (Burrows 2001). To this end, there will be a need for governments to provide policy frameworks for job creation, fair taxation, decent welfare provision and other measures.

In that context, an environmentally sustainable global economy constitutes a major source of new job creation. According to estimates by the Worldwatch Institute a few years ago, creating an environmentally sustainable economy had already generated an estimated 14 million jobs worldwide, with the promise of millions more in coming decades. Examples of figures and estimates published around the turn of the century include (Renner 2000, Worldwatch Institute 2000):

❑ It was estimated that, wind power could employ some 1.7 million people worldwide by 2020;

❑ The global recycling industry, with an annual turnover of US$160 billion, already employed more than 1.5 million people;

❑ In the United Kingdom, it was estimated that more than 700,000 additional jobs could be created over eight years by shifting the tax burden from labour to environmental damage;

❑ In the United States, product remanufacturing was already a US$53 billion per year business employing some 480,000 people directly – twice the number of jobs in the US steel industry;

❑ It was estimated that cost-effective energy efficiency measures could create almost 1.1 million net jobs in the United States over 15 to 20 years.

Currently, in the United States, occupations directly associated with preserving the natural environment and carrying out relevant research represent more than 500,000 jobs (US Department of Labor 2006).

Beyond new employment opportunities, moving towards a more environmentally friendly and sustainable global economical model represents an opportunity to contribute to poverty reduction and to tackle related issues, such as how the benefits of free trade are distributed.

The multiple and complex articulation of the need for environmental protection, decent employment and poverty reduction also has human rights and human development dimensions, as reflected in the Millennium Development Goals.

Ensuring environmental sustainability, including sustainable access to safe drinking water, contributes to the eradication of extreme poverty and hunger, as people largely depend on natural resources in their daily lives. Likewise, poverty reduction provides a positive basis for both employment and environmental protection through (among other factors) improved education, increased gender equality and the empowerment of women. In 2000-04 only two-thirds of women in the least developed and landlocked developing countries were literate. In 2005 women still occupied less than 16 per cent of parliamentary seats globally (UN Statistics Division 2006). Significant improvements thus need to be made in the areas of education and gender equality, with a view to expanding both decent employment and sustainable development.

Frequently, "working environments" and "living environments" are common or overlap significantly. One of the best known examples is Bhopal, India. In 1984, 27 tonnes of poison gas (methyl isocyanate, or MIC) escaped from a Union Carbide pesticide factory in Bhopal. Half a million people, many of whom lived in shanty towns in the factory area, were exposed to the gas; an estimated 15,000 to 33,000 died from cancers and other diseases related to MIC exposure. Deaths reportedly continue to occur at a rate of one per day. More than 120 000 people still suffer from the effects of the accident and subsequent soil and water pollution. Their ailments include blindness, extreme breathing difficulties and gynecological disorders. There is a high incidence not only of cancers, but also of brain damage and birth defects (BBC 2004, Bhopal Medical Appeal and Sambhavna Trust, Edwards, Palash 2006, Sinha 2003).[17]

Transferring obsolete or dangerous technologies, products or waste to other countries often has harmful effects on the health of workers and their communities, raising the issue of human rights and the "right to a standard of living adequate for health and well-being" (Universal Declaration of Human Rights, Article 25). In such cases, measures adopted to protect the environment address both human development and poverty issues.

---

17   Dow Chemical bought Union Carbide in 2001, "thereby acquiring its assets and responsibilities. However Dow Chemical has steadfastly refused to clean up the site, provide safe drinking water, compensate the victims, or disclose the composition of the gas leak, information that doctors could use to properly treat the victims." Excerpted from Bhopal Medical Appeal and Sambhavna Trust website. Dow and Union Carbide deny these accusations (see, for example, BBC 2004).

Improved health and living conditions provide the fundamental conditions for sustained economic and human development. In 2002 almost two-thirds of the global rural population still had no access to improved sanitation and 28 per cent did not have sustainable access to an improved water source (UN Statistics Division 2006).

As stated in the eighth Millennium Development Goal, a global partnership for development entails making decent and productive work available to youth, particularly in developing countries, and making available the benefits of new technologies, especially ICT – both of which are prerequisites for further sustainable economic development.

Addressing environmental, economic and human development issues together offers interesting synergies. Measures adopted in one area may have an impact, positive or negative, in another area. In this regard, the interests of trade unions and workers complement environmental protection goals and, more generally, sustainable development objectives very well.

Trade unions and workers: natural allies for achieving sustainable development

While the nine major groups identified in Agenda 21 (women; children and youth; indigenous people and their communities; non-governmental organizations (NGOs); local authorities; workers and trade unions; business and industry; the scientific and technological community farmers) need to continue to improve their understanding of each other's priorities, building on the strengths of each group provides interesting and encouraging perspectives that can help to achieve sustainable development.

Trade unions are well-positioned to proactively identify problems – and to be part of the solution – by sharing their knowledge and experience. Furthermore, they can play a significant role in stimulating research and development aimed at, for example, cleaner production.

With over 200 years of experience in protecting workers' rights, trade unions can make the environment a focus of collective bargaining (one of the most important tools for realizing corporate social responsibility), advocate more sensitive methods of using natural resources, and promote benefit-sharing and access to information and justice. Political lobbying, campaigning, and reaching out to communities with respect to sustainable consumption and production are additional ways to move towards sustainable development.

Environmental policies that integrate workers' needs and perspectives, will help in reaching just employment transition. Environmentalists, in cooperation with workers, have a critical role to play in increasing awareness of environmental challenges and building workers' capacity to implement relevant provisions of environmental conventions, legislation and policies.

The labour and environmental communities should no longer be viewed as living in different worlds. The goals of the labour and environmental movements are mutually dependent. Creating jobs in the long term requires a sound natural environment, while effective environmental policies rely on the support and involvement of workers.

In view of the growing understanding of the shared interests of the labour and environmental communities, it is becoming evident that the labour movement can be a strong partner and a political ally of the environmental movement through pushing for the policy changes that are urgently needed to foster the transition to an environmentally sustainable global economy, thus overcoming some of the political differences of the past. At the same time, the environmental community can be an ally of the labour movement in promoting adherence to basic labour rights. By working together, the labour and environmental movements can create sustainable jobs that are good for the health of the planet and of those who inhabit it.

References

- BBC (2004). Television and radio reports on the 20th anniversary of the Bhopal disaster, including the version presented by Dow and Union Carbide (http://news.bbc.co.uk/1/hi/programmes/bhopal/).

- Bhopal Medical Appeal and Sambhavna Trust (undated website). What happened in Bhopal? (www.bhopal.org/whathappened.html).

- Burrows, Mae (2001). Just Transition. Alternatives Journal 27:1.

- Edwards, Tim (undated website). How many died in Bhopal? (open letter to the Houston Chronicle) (www.bhopal.net/oldstie/death-toll.html).

- Fussler, Claude (2004). Responsible Excellence Pays!, Greenleaf Publishing, Sheffield, UK.

- Heal, Geoffrey (2005). The Costs of Inaction with Respect to Biodiversity Loss. OECD Environment Policy Committee (EPOC) High-level Special Session on the Costs of Inaction.

- ILO (International Labour Organization) (2001). The Size of the Working Poor Population in Developing Countries (by Nomaan Majid). ILO Employment Paper 2001/16 (www-ilo-mirror. cornell.edu/public/english/employment/strat/publ/ep01-16.htm).

— (2004-05). World Employment Report 2004-05 (www.ilo.org/public/english/employment/strat/ wer2004.htm)

— (2006). Global Employment Trends Brief, January 2006 (www.ilo.org/public/english/employment/ strat/download/getb06en.pdf).

(...cont'd)

References (...cont'd)

- Millennium Ecosystem Assessment (2005). Ecosystems and Human Well-Being, Opportunities and Challenges for Business and Industry.

- Morgenstern, Richard D., William A. Pizer and Shih Jhih-Shyang (2002). Jobs Versus the Environment: An Industry-Level Perspective. Journal of Environmental Economics and Management 43:412-36.

- Palash, Kumar (2006). Bhopal Gas Victims in Long Walk for Clean Water. Reuters news service, 30 March.

- Renner, Michael (2000). Working for the Environment: A Growing Source of Jobs. Worldwatch Paper 152.

- Sinha, Indra (2003). Bhopal: Holding Corporate Terrorists Accountable (www.alternet.org/story/15845).

- Stern, Nicholas (2006). Stern Review: The Economics of Climate Change, Executive Summary (http://www.hm-treasury.gov.uk/Independent_Reviews/stern_review_economics_climate_change/sternreview_index.cfm).
  UNEP (United Nations Environment Programme) (2002). Global Environment Outlook (GEO-3) (www.unep.org/geo/geo3).

- UNEP Finance Initiative (2002). Climate Risk to Global Economy, CEO Briefing, A document of the UNEP FI Climate Change Working Group.

— (2005). The Future of Climate Policy, The Financial Sector Perspective, CEO Briefing, A document of the UNEP FI Climate Change Working Group.

- United Nations Statistics Division (2006). Millennium Indicators Database, 9 May (on-line) (http://unstats.un.org).

- United States Department of Labor, Bureau of Labor Statistics (2006). Occupational Outlook Handbook, 10 May (on-line) (www.bls.gov).

- Wagner, Thomas (2005). Environmental policy and the equilibrium rate of unemployment. Journal of Environmental Economics and Management, 49132-56.

- Worldwatch Institute (2000). Saving the Environment: A Jobs Engine for the 21st Century (press release). 21 September.

2. Participating at All Levels

Lene Olsen, *Bureau for Workers' Activities, International Labour Organization*

© *Mark Edwards / UNEP*

Electrical factory, Columbia: *Better job opportunities have increased independence for many women and have given them a new status and role in their families and society. Women continue to have lower participation rates in the labour market, higher unemployment rates, and significant pay differences in most regions.*

2.1. Workers in the workplace and in their communities

Ever since workers started to organize and to form trade unions, the trade union movement has been involved in addressing socio-economic issues and has contributed to the improvement of the working and living conditions of workers. Initially, trade unions were mainly concerned with issues closely related to the individual workplace – which were often linked to problems in the surrounding community. However, very soon their agenda also included issues at the national and international level.

There is still a lot for workers and their trade unions to do to improve basic working and living conditions for women and men all over the world. In addition, new and important issues have emerged during the last 30 years in an increasingly integrated world. Growing environmental concerns are among these issues. With respect to trade union involvement in environmental matters, there is no doubt that trade union-led improvements have been made, and that these improvements have often been as successful as other trade union initiatives in the past. Trade unions' part in improving occupational health and safety in many countries is an example. There is a strong connection between defending *health and safety at the workplace* and defending the *local (and wider) environment* (Box 2.1.1).

Box 2.1.1

Côte d'Ivoire: Hazardous waste dumping threatens health and safety and the environment

On 19 August 2006, up to 500 tonnes of toxic waste was dumped in Abidjan, the largest city of Côte d'Ivoire (Ivory Coast), by the Probo Koala, a ship registered in Panama and chartered by a Dutch company. Consisting mainly of gasoline, water and caustic soda, this waste was discovered at several locations around the city, including roadsides, open ground and a channel leading to a lake. The circumstances under which the waste was transferred from the Probo Koala remain unclear. The company claims tankers belonging to a local company accepted it, with the understanding that appropriate treatment and disposal would be carried out.

Some ten people died after inhaling toxic fumes, and thousands of others sought medical treatment. One of the substances to which they appear to have been exposed is hydrogen sulphide, a poisonous gas. Symptoms included nausea, headaches, eye and throat irritation, and breathing and stomach problems. Secondary exposures via surface water, groundwater and the food chain were possible (some livestock culling took place).[18] Members of the Ivorian government were forced to resign, as the Probo Koala incident was widely considered to result from local corruption.

This incident focused attention on the illegal transport of hazardous waste from industrialized to developing countries, and on the international agreements[19] regulating such transport (BBC News 2006, Greenpeace 2006, Sustainlabour 2006, Wikipedia 2006).

---

18 By December 2006, arrangements had been made for 7 500 tonnes of contaminated soil to be treated at an incineration plant in France (Bertrand Olivier, "L'Isère brule de questions autour des déchets d'Abidjan," Libération, Paris, France, 5 December 2006). This article reported that 100 000 people were given medical treatment following the Probo Koala incident
19 The Basel Convention on the Control of Transboundary Movements of Hazardous Wastes and Their Disposal ("the Basel Convention"), which entered into force in 1992 (www.basel.int), and the OECD Decision on Transboundary Movements of Waste Destined for Recovery Operations, adopted in 2001 (www2.oced.org/waste/).

When trade unions become involved with environmental issues at the workplace, they use existing tools and structures, such as social dialogue and collective bargaining, awareness raising campaigns and solidarity projects. Their work on traditional issues such as employment and occupational health and safety has led to healthier workplaces. However, trade unions are increasingly looking at the wider environmental implications of production and the need to promote a sustainable development agenda that goes beyond the workplace – an agenda covering, for instance, the effects of production on climate change.

Using traditional tools and structures to address environmental issues

In many parts of the world, trade unions are using their traditional collective bargaining skills to deal with environmental issues (Box 2.1.2). Especially when they address environmental concerns at the workplace which have financial implications, trade unions can ensure that profit maximization (the main objective of entrepreneurial activities) does not lead to disregard for potential damage to workers' health or to the environment.

Many companies and employers' organizations have produced environmental statements and policies that demonstrate their commitment to address environmental issues. Some have been negotiated at national level, between unions and industry or employers' federations; others have been designed for implementation at the individual workplace level (ILO 1993). Numerous collective agreements, including "green" clauses, have also been signed, as have specific "green agreements" at the local and national level. The aim of all these agreements is to set out commitments on environmental issues, identify each partner's responsibilities under the agreements, identify procedures, and create a structure for working on common priorities and a policy on environmental issues.

At the workplace level environmental issues can include purchasing and recycling policies aimed at environmental protection. Such policies favour, among other things, low-energy lighting, low fuel-consuming vehicles, biodegradable cleaning materials, wood from environmentally well-managed forests, recycled paper and the elimination of excessive packaging (ILO 1993).

With globalization, many national enterprises have developed into multinationals. To ensure that workers' rights and working conditions are respected in all the workplaces of multinational enterprises, many International Framework Agreements (IFAs) have been negotiated and signed between multinational companies and the trade unions representing their workforces, which are themselves represented by individual Global Union Federations (GUFs). An example of a full-fledged collective bargaining agreement at the international level is that negotiated by the International Maritime Employers' Committee (IMEC), a group of ship owners/ship managers, with the International Transport Workers' Federation (ITF). This agreement includes provisions on wages, hours and working conditions aboard ships, including health and safety protection (Lillie 2004).

Box 2.1.2

Canada: Extended Producer Responsibility (EPR) – making environment a workers' issue in the automobile industry [20]

Workers in the automobile industry, as well as management, need to be involved in decision-making regarding the type of products to build and the environmental soundness of the production process.

The Canadian Auto Workers Union (CAW) has experimented with the use of collective bargaining as a tool to provide a voice for workers on environmental issues in and out of the workplace. Emphasizing the need to establish and strengthen workers' right to bargain with employers on environmental issues, they have demonstrated the need to challenge management's control of decision-making on environmental matters and to involve the public in campaigns to promote environmental concerns in the community.

In 2003 the union's activities built on the concept of Extended Producer Responsibility (EPR). Where EPR is in effect, vehicles at the end of their life-cycle are returned to manufacturers for safe environmental disposal or the recovery of useable parts. EPR, which represents an environmentally friendly source of employment, requires the following:

- Producers are responsible for a number of the environmental impacts of their products throughout these products' life cycle;

- Producers take back products at the end of their useful lives;

- Products must be re-used or recycled, rather than incinerated or sent to landfill.

Although EPR has been established in Europe, North American car manufacturers continue to resist taking on this obligation. The Canadian Auto Workers Union has tried to bring about change through public campaigns, political lobbying and direct negotiations.[21]

20 Based on the case study presented by Nick De Carlo, representing the Canadian Auto Workers Union (CAW), at the Trade Union Assembly on Labour and the Environment / WILL 2006.

21 "There is substantial economic and environmental opportunity in 'mining' waste. It results, for example, in reductions in energy and resource use, and in the development of new products and new product design. There are also job advantages for workers because disassembly is, in general, more labour intensive than assembly. But EPR has to be done the right way. Reuse and recycling have to be promoted over shredding or incineration. Toxins have to be removed, both from the final product and the production process. Design for disassembly has to be encouraged. And, in Canada, in particular, mechanisms have to be put in place to ensure that we develop and promote the economic infrastructure to reuse and recycle materials. This means expansion of our manufacturing base, which in turn means new economic opportunities for Canada." Excerpted from "The Environment is a Tough Issue for Unions," Canadian Auto Workers (CAW) website, 7 June 2004 (www.caw.ca/news/natpostbuzz/buzznat_060704.asp).

An IFA signed between the International Federation of Chemical, Energy, Mine and General Workers' Unions (ICEM), and supported by its French affiliates Fedechemie (CGT-FO) and the Fédération Chemie Energie (CFDT) as well as the French specialty chemicals company, Rhodia,[24] includes clauses on the environment. As a supporter of the UN Global Compact,[25] Rhodia is committed to respect all of the Compact's ten principles, including Principle 7 on the environment. These principles are highlighted in

24 www.rhodia.com.

25 The Global Compact, initiated in 1999 by UN Secretary-General Kofi Annan, brings companies together with UN agencies to support universal environmental and social principles. Companies from all regions of the world, as well as business associations, trade union bodies and international NGOs, have committed themselves to advance the Global Compact's ten universal principles in the areas of human rights, labour, the environment and anti-corruption (www.unglobalcompact.org). Also see section 4.2, "Corporate social responsibility and accountability" by Cornis Lugt, Gerd Albracht, Daniela Zampini and Corey Kaplan, especially Box 4.2.2.

the agreement; there are also special paragraphs on risk management and environmental protection. The paragraph under the heading "Environment" states that Rhodia complies with national and international environmental laws and regulations and adheres to "the chemical industry's commitment to progress in environmental protection."

Moreover, the company applies these principles based on its ongoing commitment to improve safety and health and environmental protection and to preserve natural resources. Employee awareness of relevant environmental standards and company policies plays an important role in Rhodia's approach at both the international and local levels. Rhodia and ICEM will combine their efforts to enhance employee awareness and expertise in the area of environmental protection.[26]

The purpose of both national collective agreements and IFAs is to improve workers' living conditions and conditions at the workplace. However, the success of any agreement depends on union strength. Full implementation of any agreement is only possible when workers are organized into free trade unions and are able to bargain collectively at all levels. Respect for fundamental principles and rights at work, especially those set out in ILO Conventions No. 87 and 98, is essential. These two conventions deal with the right to freedom of association and the right to organize and bargain collectively. They are two of the most important ILO conventions and are those most valued by workers everywhere:

26   www.icem.org//files/PDF/Global_agreements_pdfs/RhodiaEN.pdf

Box 2.1.3

International Framework Agreements (IFAs)

International Framework Agreements are representative of an emerging form of industrial relations. IFAs are signed between multinational enterprises and Global Union Federations (GUFs) representing workers in their sectors and companies. They contain a commitment to honour trade union rights; many also contain references to some or all of the fundamental rights enshrined in the ILO Declaration on Fundamental Principles and Rights at Work.[22]

Several IFAs refer to issues covered by other ILO conventions, including in the health and safety area. Unlike unilaterally adopted "codes of conduct" for a company or companies (which often seek to demonstrate the virtue of the companies' behaviour), IFAs recognize that problems are likely to arise within the often vast operations of multinational enterprises. Thus they provide a mechanism for addressing and, often, resolving such problems.

Some agreements seek to encourage suppliers and subcontractors to apply the same standards to their operations. For example, an agreement signed between IKEA and the Building and Wood Workers' International (BWI) applies exclusively to suppliers.[23]

International Framework Agreements are designed to facilitate the resolution of problems, primarily at the national level. While they help to create a climate for negotiating collective bargaining agreements, they are not a substitute for these agreements.

A number of IFAs include clauses on the protection of nature and the environment, with monitoring carried out by trade union affiliates around the world.

22   The Declaration on Fundamental Principles and Rights at Work was adopted by the International Labour Conference in June 1998. It commits ILO Member States to respect and promote principles and rights in four categories (whether or not they have ratified the relevant conventions). These categories are: freedom of association and the effective recognition of the right to collective bargaining; elimination of forced or compulsory labour; abolition of child labour; and elimination of discrimination in respect of employment and occupation (ILO 1998).
23   www.bwint.org/default.asp?Index=46&language=EN

❑ *Convention No. 87 on Freedom of Association and Protection of the Right to Organize* aims to provide workers with the right to form their own trade unions or organizations and to join them freely. It also aims to guarantee that these organizations can function without interference from the public authorities (ILO 1948);

❑ *Convention No. 98 on the Right to Organize and Collective Bargaining* aims to protect workers against acts of anti-union discrimination, safeguarding their organizations from interference by employers' organizations and promoting voluntary collective bargaining (ILO 1949).

Of the 178 ILO Member States, 147 and 156, respectively, had ratified Conventions No. 87 and No. 98 as of 6 May 2006. However, violations of these conventions still exist, impeding effective trade union participation in many countries. Suppressing the possibility for workers' interests to be properly represented means that serious workplace problems, including environmental ones, are often ignored until severe and long-lasting damage makes it impossible to deny their existence, even in repressive societies.

Violations of trade union rights are symptomatic of unsustainable forms of development. It is important for trade union rights to be respected, so that workers can contribute to the environmentally sustainable development agenda and address these issues at the workplace as soon as they occur.

In the Final Resolution adopted in January 2006 by the Trade Union Assembly on Labour and the Environment / WILL 2006, the importance of fundamental principles and rights at work was reiterated. Participants agreed (Trade Union Assembly on Labour and the Environment 2006b):

❑ To integrate the environmental and social dimensions of sustainable development with a rights-based approach. Fundamental rights of workers such as freedom of association and collective bargaining must be respected if workers and their unions are to be able to engage in strategies for sustainable development. Moreover, human rights must include the universal, equitable, egalitarian and environmentally sound access to basic resources such as water and energy;[27]

❑ To enhance the dialogue between labour and management, consultation and negotiation in the workplace on sustainable development, and social dialogue at the sectoral, national and international levels in both public and private sectors, to use appropriate tools to increase social and environmental responsibility and accountability of enterprises through both trade union and multi-stakeholder participation in genuine initiatives and to ensure that corporate social responsibility involves both compliance with law and voluntary initiatives.[28]

Campaigns and awareness raising on environmental issues

Trade union campaigns and awareness raising are normally built around specific issues. This approach has also been used in relation to environmental issues perceived by workers and their trade unions to be urgent or worthy of being promoted.

---

27   Article 1(b).
28   Article 1(h).

One outcome of the project has been increased awareness among agricultural workers, particularly regarding pesticides' impact on health and the environment. More cases of chemical poisoning have been reported to national authorities than previously, and national legislation has been reviewed, with worker participation. There has also been increased recognition of unions and workers at relevant national and international forums.

One such issue is exposure to pesticides (Box 2.1.4). In this regard, it is particularly important to raise awareness of gender-related differences in pesticides' health impacts. Women have different body weights, body masses, fat-to-muscle ratios, hormonal systems and reproductive functions than men, among other differences. Because they have a higher percentage of body fat than men, especially in the breasts, they are at greater risk of harm from potentially hazardous chemicals. They are more vulnerable to certain exposures during puberty, pregnancy, menopause and old age.

Box 2.1.4

The Global Pesticides Project[29]

The Global Pesticides Project was begun in 1998 by the International Union of Food, Agricultural, Hotel, Restaurant, Catering, Tobacco and Allied Workers Associations (IUF). An initiative between the IUF, the Swedish Agricultural Workers' Union, and agricultural unions in Ghana, Malawi, Uganda, United Republic of Tanzania and Zimbabwe, it was mainly aimed at:

- Identifying and phasing out the most hazardous pesticides;

- Protecting workers' health, particularly the health of vulnerable groups such as pregnant women, spray teams and the elderly;

- Environmental protection.

---

29 Based on the case study presented by Yahya Msangi, representing the International Union of Food, Agricultural, Hotel, Restaurant, Catering, Tobacco and Allied Workers Associations (IUF), at the Trade Union Assembly on Labour and the Environment / WILL 2006.

Gender differences in the effects of pesticide exposure are increasingly being acknowledged.[30] Women are also more likely than men to work in the service sector (e.g. as cleaners, in hair and beauty salons or in caring industries) and to be exposed to hazardous chemicals there. In the tourism industry women are often employed by hotels and restaurants, where they come into contact with hazardous chemicals including solvents. Moreover, women's traditional role in the home often increases such exposures (Ransom 2002, WEN 2005).

---

30 "Pesticide use and exposure among women is a central issue in the move towards a sustainable future…Better understanding of the gender implications of pesticide use include: • Ways in which women are exposed to pesticides in agricultural production, as well as different patterns of pesticide use between women and men; • Unique health impacts of pesticides on women. The extent of information to women about pesticides increases understanding of the impacts of use and increases agricultural practices and consumer habits which reduce exposures. When women are exposed, so too are children through women's breast milk contamination and because women play an important role in educating children. Women are also often the ones responsible when other family members are impacted by illnesses due to pesticide exposure. Several of the recommendations in Agenda 21 relate to women and pesticide use. In Chapter 14, there are recommendations that there should be increased public awareness of sustainable agriculture in women's groups, that governments should disseminate to farming households more information involving 'reduced use of agricultural chemicals' and train women's groups, farmers and extension agents in alternative non-chemical ways of controlling pests that are of significance. Economic considerations must be taken into account related to the costs to women of health problems due to exposures to pesticides both for themselves and the family as well as the issues of women as consumers of pesticide products." Excerpted from Ransom 2002.

Awareness raising at the workplace not only benefits the worker or workplace, but also society in general, including across national bor-ders. By increasing awareness among their members, trade unions increase citizen awareness and can contribute, in turn, to the modification of personal behaviour with respect to the environment. There is much that everyone – workers and others – can do to promote environmental awareness. Practical steps that everyone can take (at home and at the workplace) include saving electricity; recycling paper, metal, glass and other materials; insisting that local authorities take appropriate actions; using environmentally friendly products; campaigning for better public transport; and taking part in the work of environmental organizations. By playing their personal roles in this way, individuals can help to create a healthier environment for themselves, their fellow human beings and the planet (ILO 1993).

Solidarity and knowledge transfer

According to ILO figures (ILO 2006), 2.85 billion people aged 15 years and older were in work at the end of 2005. This is 1.5 per cent more than in 2004, and represents an increase of more than 16.5 per cent since 1995. Of the 2.8 billion workers in the world in 2005, nearly 1.4 billion did not earn enough to lift themselves and their families above the US$2 a day poverty line – the same number of people as ten years earlier. Among these working poor, more than half a billion lived with their families in extreme poverty on less than US$1 per person per day.[31]

Both industrialized and developing countries need to improve their environmental attitudes. However, developing and enforcing environmental measures in very poor countries can be difficult without the resources, trained personnel and know-how found in industrialized countries. Moreover, global environmental problems are largely caused by industrialized countries, which are increasingly being joined by the fast-growing developing countries. These problems will have their worst impact on those developing countries which are the least able to prevent or adapt to change (ILO 1993).

Here again, there is a gender dimension. Women are more likely than men to be poor and to live in poor environments, e.g. near polluting factories or waste sites or in high-traffic areas exposed to automobile pollution and other hazards. To address these differences, solidarity projects and knowledge sharing (which are part of the work carried out by trade unions worldwide) are necessary.

The Norwegian/Russian trade union programme supporting cleaner production and occupational health, safety and environment (OHSE) in Russian industries demonstrates the value of such knowledge transfer (Box 2.1.5).

Job creation and just transition: processes that begin at the workplace

Workers and their trade unions not only want to be able to influence the way their company or organization affects their workplaces, lives, and surrounding communities and environment. They also want to influence how their employment is directly affected. They are concerned about the way workplaces are managed, how commercial risks are taken, and how these activities may eventually threaten employment.

---

31   See Chapter 1, "Labour and the Environment: A Natural Synergy" by Sophie De Coninck and Hilary French.

Box 2.1.5

Norway and Russia: A partnership programme to promote knowledge sharing on cleaner production and OHSE issues [32]

The Norwegian Confederation of Trade Unions – Landsorganisasjonen i Norge (LO Norway) – and the Federation of Independent Trade Unions of Russia (FNPR) initiated a partnership programme to promote cleaner production in Russian industries by transferring knowledge from Norway to Russia. The partnership also involved the Norwegian Society of Chartered Technical and Scientific Professionals (Tekna) and Russian local and regional authorities. The programme's main objectives were:

- To improve working conditions and reduce emissions and wastes;

- To increase workers' knowledge, competence and involvement in cleaner production and occupational health, safety and environment (OHSE) issues, as well as establishing in-company systems for continual improvement;

- To convince business actors that cleaner production constitutes a win-win solution, as it satisfies environmental standards while it reduces production costs.

A six-month training course was conducted within the framework of the programme. At the end of this course, participants (workers, engineers and representatives of middle management) presented a final project report.

The report's main findings were that the programme gave an impetus to workers' knowledge, competence and involvement with respect to health, safety and environmental challenges at workplaces, in company towns, and in the Arctic environment. Knowledge transfer through the presentation of Norwegian examples and practices was particularly beneficial to participants. The introduction of one or two new programmes is planned.

---

32 Based on the case study presented by Halvor Woien, representing LO Norway and FNPR, at the Trade Union Assembly on Labour and the Environment / WILL 2006.

Through ensuring *decent work* trade unions also promote environmentally sustainable employment. Within the ILO, the following characteristics have been cited in defining "decent work":

- ❏ It is productive and secure;
- ❏ It ensures respect of labour rights;
- ❏ It provides an adequate income;
- ❏ It offers social protection ;
- ❏ It includes social dialogue, union freedom, collective bargaining and participation.

Ensuring decent work is an important part of achieving not only *sustainable employment*, but *environmentally sustainable employment*.

Clearly it will be necessary to develop new, non-polluting industries in order to create a more environmentally sustainable world economy. New alternative energy sources and alternative forms of agriculture can produce new employment opportunities. Developments in other fields (e.g. recycling and pollution prevention) can also contribute to the creation of new jobs. However, this does not necessarily mean that when old polluting industries close down, workers in those industries will be transferred directly to new jobs. Jobs may be lost in one geographical area and created in another, or even lost in one specific industrial sector and not replaced with jobs in the same sector. This will result in job insecurity for some workers. Not everybody will have the possibility to move or to convert their skills to a new sector immediately. For that reason, it is important to involve workers and their trade unions in the process of change.

The involvement of workers starts at the workplace. It is at this level that experience will be gained, and that it will often be possible to develop new ideas and alternatives. Workers have valuable "on-site" knowledge which should be taken into account when policies are developed at different levels. Through planning, education and preparation of changes in cooperation with employers, governments and communities, a "just transition" from unsustainable industries to more sustainable ones – socially, economically and environmentally – may be carried out more fairly and efficiently.

Respect for and implementation of the ILO conventions that secure workers' right to participation are essential. Top-down, centralized decision-making not only excludes workers from the process of change; it also turns potential cooperation into resistance, as workers have their fill of action plans and policies initiated without any apparent concern for them. What is required, trade unions say, is a shift to participatory management of change, which values worker innovation, empowerment and responsibility, and an acceptance of fundamental rights and freedoms, as defined in the ILO's Convention on Fundamental Rights and Freedoms at Work (ILO 1998), including freedom of association (Gereluk and Royer 2001).

Conventions dealing with employment policies and income security are also relevant to "just transition" measures. Article 3 of ILO Convention No. 122 (the Employment Policy Convention) specifies that in applying this Convention, representatives of the persons affected by the measures to be taken, and particularly representatives of employers and workers, shall be consulted concerning employment policies with a view to taking fully into account their experience and views and securing their full cooperation in formulating and enlisting support for such policies (ILO 1964).

Health, safety and environment at the workplace

Health and safety issues have always been the most natural link between trade unions and environmental issues. This important link was highlighted in the Final Resolution of the Nairobi Trade Union Assembly / WILL 2006. The meeting agreed (Resolution 2006b):

> To link occupational health to environmental and public health policy and practice; while raising standards of occupational health and safety as an objective in its own right, to reinforce the International Labour Organization conventions and programmes to develop and promote it; to take account of the need for differentiated approaches between developed and developing countries; to use this as a central element of campaigns to fight HIV/AIDS; to prevent worker death, injury and illness from the effects of chemicals or dangerous substances, such as asbestos; and to ensure the right to reproductive health for women and men.[33]

At many workplaces around the world, joint trade union/employer committee structures have been created to bring about occupational health and safety changes. Little by little, these structures have also begun to be used to address environmental issues at the workplace. The tools for auditing, assessing, monitoring, record-keeping, evaluating

---

33   Article 1(j).

and making changes to promote worker safety can now be applied to questions that reach beyond, into the realms of environmental protection, pubic health and employer accountability, touching upon a broad range of issues including most recently, HIV/AIDS (Trade Union Assembly on Labour and the Environment 2006a).

Where joint workplace structures are weak or non-existent, awareness raising and the promotion of such structures may be carried out by trade unions (Box 2.1.6).

Box 2.1.6

Asia: OHSE and corporate social responsibility - vehicles for organizing and social dialogue[34]

Trade union organizations in Bangladesh, Indonesia, Pakistan and Philippines have been working together to promote worker participation in OHSE issues, create OHSE units within national centres, and develop union policies, programmes and objectives, in cooperation with the Asian Workers Occupational Health, Safety and Environment Institute (OSHEI) in Bangkok, Thailand.

The objectives of OSHEI are to strengthen local capacities in occupational health, safety and environment and corporate social responsibility, and to engage unions in dialogue. Asia is characterized by high rates of workplace accidents and fatalities, outdated workplace laws, poor regulatory enforcement, and a large informal economic sector. In a two-phase programme, the Institute first developed a toolkit for intervention, as well as groups trained on occupational health, safety and environmental issues; the second phase involved implementing the toolkit in study circles where larger numbers of workers were trained. Intervention tools were research and documentation, awareness raising, advocacy, networking, dissemination of information, training and fundraising. The thematic issues addressed were:

- Chemical risks: hazardous substances in the workplace;
- Trade union actions to obtain equal and sustainable access to resources and services;
- Occupational, environmental and public health: asbestos and HIV/AIDS campaigns;
- Corporate social responsibility and accountability.

In the Institute's model for social partnership there are four actors: governments with regulatory powers; NGOs monitoring social conditions; workers engaged in production; and employers supplying resources.

Participating organizations' co-ordinators are trained on OHSE, corporate social responsibility (CSR) and project implementation, as well as on work plan development and timelines for possible intervention at the local level. Where trade unions are involved in advocacy at the local level, this process is called "socialization". One national co-ordinator and four resource persons from the participating organizations in each country are trained to form the critical mass for implementing relevant interventions at the local level, with a view to influencing members.

---

34 Based on the case study presented by Ng Wei Khiang, Director, Asian Workers Occupational Health, Safety and Environment Institute (OSHEI), at the Trade Union Assembly on Labour and the Environment / WILL 2006.

Joint workplace initiatives by trade unions and employers to monitor and report on workplace activities are based on a framework set out in ILO Convention No. 155 concerning Occupational Safety and Health and the Working Environment, which provides for (ILO 1981):

- Cooperation at the workplace between workers and employers, as jointly responsible for the work environment (e.g. through joint health and safety committees);
- Workers' right to refuse unsafe and unhealthy work;
- Workers' right to information and training;
- Specific government provision for health and safety in the form of health and safety legislation and regulations;
- Devotion of government resources to health and safety;
- An inspectorate.

It has been shown that one of the most effective means of reducing injury and illness is to involve workers and their representatives in all aspects of health and safety through a health and safety regime, as envisioned by the ILO. The same principles might be valid for environmental protection at the workplace level (Box 2.1.7).

Leveraging workers' experience for sustainable development

This chapter has looked at a few of the many activities being carried out by workers and their representatives at workplace level to improve the environment. It has also provided a short overview of some of the traditional tools used for (and issues linked to) sustainable development activities. In work on relatively "new" issues focusing on the environment, the "old" preconditions for workers' involvement are the same: they include respect for rights (national and international) related to freedom of association, collective bargaining, and health and safety. Not only are the preconditions the same, but activities concerned with the "old" issues are greatly furthering the sustainable development agenda. When the term "sustainable development" was introduced, it was defined as development that "meets the needs of the present without compromising the ability of future generations to meet their own needs" (WCED 1987).

Trade unions' work to promote better working and living conditions for women and men is very much about promoting economic, social and environmental sustainable development. That is why trade unions' involvement at the workplace is so crucial.[35]

Although high-level meetings and conferences at the national and international level have reiterated the importance of trade union involvement at the workplace, barriers still persist and trade union involvement with respect to the environmental agenda is sometimes still difficult.

In this regard, implementation of ILO standards becomes highly relevant to work on sustainable development issues – especially in relation to its core conventions on freedom of association and the right to collective bargaining, but also to other conventions (particularly those on health and safety). The ILO's primary goal is decent work, which it defines as "access for all to enable people to meet their basic economic, social and

---

35 "The notion that sustainable development threatens jobs and creates unfair competition persists to this day. One objective for trade unions is to dispel this notion. Indeed, jobs will be lost but transitional programmes can be instituted as set out in Chapter 29 of Agenda 21 to ensure that changes do not disrupt effective implementation of sustainable development programs. In the five years following the 1992 Rio Earth Summit, trade unions developed possible Just Transition scenarios that all stakeholders should consider in order for sustainable development initiatives to be successful. And since 1999 there has been a focus on how to complement these policy developments with workplace-based activities for workers at the production level." Excerpted from Two Years Since Johannesburg: The Follow-up from a Labour Perspective, Sustainlabour, 2004, p. 2.

family needs and responsibilities and an adequate level of social protection for worker and family members."[36] This will help people to "meet the needs of the present without compromising the ability of future generations to meet their own needs."

By furthering decent work at the workplace and promoting International Labour Standards, workers are contributing substantially to the sustainable development agenda.

---

36 "The primary goal of the ILO is to secure decent work for women and men everywhere. It is the most widespread need, shared by people, families and communities in every society, and at all levels of development. Decent work is a global demand today, confronting political and business leadership worldwide. Much of our common future – including sustainable development – depends on how we meet this challenge." Excerpted Mwamadzingo 2006, p. 2.

Box 2.1.7

The Nigeria Labour Congress campaign for safety at the workplace and environmental protection [37]

The Nigeria Labour Congress (NLC) has initiated a project aimed to promote safety in the workplace and to protect the environment by ensuring, among other things, that:

- Collective bargaining includes environmental considerations;
- Workers receive equal pay for equal work;
- Workers are guaranteed a safe working environment;
- Health and safety laws are reviewed by the Government;
- Workers are aware of health and safety issues in the workplace and of environmental considerations.

The project seeks to secure a cleaner environment, restore the dignity of labour, change labour relations for development and growth, minimize accidents at the workplace, and reach 5 million workers in the formal and informal sectors.

The project's action plans for 2006 and beyond include:

- Fact-finding visits to factories;
- Research, assessments and documentation concerning the types of chemicals used at workplaces;
- An information, education and communication campaign;
- Capacity-building for leadership on health and safety laws and ILO standards;
- Stakeholder conferences on health and safety and the environment.

---

37 Based on the case study presented by Bernard Ugbi, representing the Nigeria Labour Conference (NLC), at the Trade Union Assembly on Labour and the Environment / WILL 2006.

References

- BBC News website (2006). In pictures: Ivorian toxic waste (http://news.bbc.co.uk/1/hi/in_pictures/5322760.stm); Ivorian cabinet quits over waste (http://news.bbc.co.uk/go/pr/fr/-/hi/world/africa/5321272.stm); "Toxic pigs" cull in Ivory Coast (http://news.bbc.co.uk/1/hi/world/africa/6134998.stm); "Toxic waste" prisoners attacked (http://news.bbc.co.uk/go/pr/fr/-/hi/world/africa/6146298.stm).

- Canadian Auto Workers Union (CAW) website (2004). The Environment is a Tough Issue for Unions (7 June) (www.caw.ca/news/natpostbuzz/buzznat_060704.asp).

- Gereluk, Winston and L. Royer (2001). Sustainable Development of the Global Economy: A Trade Union Perspective (www.ilo.org/public/english/protection/ses/download/docs/sustain.pdf).

— (2002). Workroom versus Boardroom Approaches to Sustainable Development: Reversing the Downward Spiral. Earth Summit 2002: A New Deal. Felix Dodds and Toby Middleton (eds.). Earthscan, London.

- Greenpeace website (2006). Toxic Death Ship Blocked (www.greenpeace.org/international/news/toxic-ship-probo-koala-240906).

- ILO (International Labour Organization) (1948). Convention No. 87 concerning Freedom of Association and Protection of the Right to Organise (www.ilo.org/ilolex/english/convdisp1.htm).

— (1949). Convention No. 98 concerning the Application of the Principles of the Right to Organise and to Bargain Collectively (www.ilo.org/ilolex/english/convdisp1.htm).

— (1964). Convention No. 122 concerning Employment Policy (www.ilo.org/ilolex/english/convdisp1.htm).

— (1981). Convention No. 155 concerning Occupational Safety and Health and the Working Environment (www.ilo.org/ilolex/english/convdisp1.htm).

— (1990). Environment and the World of Work (Report of the Director-General to the International Labour Conference, 77th Session).

— (1993) Workers' Education and the Environment (special issue of Labour Education, 93-1993/4).

— (1996). Using ILO Standards to Promote Environmentally Sustainable Development (series of eight discussion booklets): 1. The ILO and Its Standards; 2. Environmental Indicators of Development; 3. Political Indicators of Development; 4. Economic Development and Security; 5. Social Development; 6. Equality of Opportunity and Treatment; 7. Education and Training; 8. International Development (www.ilo.org/public/english/dialogue/actrav/enviro/trainmat/ilostand/ilostand.htm).

— (1998). Declaration on Fundamental Principles and Rights at Work (www.ilo.org/dyn/declaris/DECLARATIONWEB.INDEXPAGE).

— (2002). Protocol of 2002 to the Occupational Safety and Health Convention, 1981 (www.ilo.org/ilolex/english/convdisp1.htm).

— (2006). Global Employment Trends Brief, January 2006 (www.ilo.org/public/english/employment/strat/download/getb06en.pdf).

- Lillie, Nathan (2004). Global Collective Bargaining on Flag of Convenience Shipping. British Journal of Industrial Relations, 42:1 (March).

References (...cont'd)

- Mwamadzingo, Mohammed (2006). The Role of Decent Work in Poverty Eradication and Environmental Protection. Paper prepared for the Trade Union Regional Conference on Labour and the Environment, COSATU House, Johannesburg, South Africa, 28 and 29 July 2006 (www.sustainlabour.org/documents/africa/ILO.pdf).

- Ransom, Pamela (Women's Environment and Development Organization, WEDO) (2002). Women, Pesticides and Sustainable Agriculture, position paper. CSD NGO Women's Caucus (www.earthsummit2002.org/wcaucus/Caucus%20Position%20Papers/agriculture/pestices1.htm).

- Sustainlabour (International Labour Foundation for Sustainable Development) (2004) Two Years Since Johannesburg: The Follow-up from a Labour Perspective (www.sustainlabour.org/documents/firstmeeting_report.pdf).

— (2006). Africa, In Focus No. 1.

- Trade Union Assembly on Labour and the Environment / WILL 2006 (2006a). The Workbook (Draft Version 8.0) (www.unep.org/labour_environment/PDFs/WorkbookEN8.pdf).

— (2006b). Final Resolution of the Trade Union Assembly at its First Meeting, Nairobi, January (www.unep.org/labour_environment/PDFs/TUALEfinalresolution-ENG.pdf).

- WCED (World Commission on Environment and Development) (1987). Our Common Future (report of Brundtland Commission). Oxford University Press, Oxford, UK. Our Common Future is downloadable as a scanned UN General Assembly document (www.are.admin.ch/imperia/md/content/are/nachhaltigeentwicklung/brundtland_bericht.pdf?PHPSESSID=226cd68bfe6fc593e202731df69702d2).

- WEN (Women's Environmental Network) (2005). Why women and the environment? Briefing.

- Wikipedia (2006). Ivory Coast toxic waste spill (http://en.wikipedia.org/wiki/2006_Ivory_Coast_toxic_waste_spill).

2.2. The trade union movement and environmental participation: shaping the change, renewing trade unionism[38]

Joaquín Nieto, International Labour Foundation for Sustainable Development (Sustainlabour)

The global energy model that will prevail from the middle of the 21st century onwards will bear little resemblance to the one that was valid in the 20th century, overly dependent as it was on fossil fuels. This will be the case as much for reasons connected to climate change (provoked by man-made emissions of CO_2 and other greenhouse gases produced by the current industrial and transportation models) as because of the depletion of petroleum reserves.

Neither is our current agri-food model sustainable: it continues to destroy forest areas and to erode fertile land to a dangerous extent; it is polluting soil and water with chemical fertilizers and pesticides; and it is drastically reducing biodiversity and fishery resources. This model has not only failed to relieve hunger in the world, but it leads to an ever less efficient diet, giving rise to serious health problems due to overweight and obesity in developed countries and in the urban populations of developing countries. The solution to hunger on the one hand, and obesity on the other, is a different agri-food model that is socially and environmentally more responsible – based on a different diet but also on the large-scale development of integrated and ecological agriculture that guarantees food security and sovereignty.

It is not sustainable, either, to engage in widespread use of the thousands of toxic chemicals that poison our rivers, soil, atmosphere and bodies and other living beings. Millions and millions of tonnes of toxic substances in workplaces cause illness and death: hundreds of thousands of workers die every year because of exposure to these substances, and millions of women workers suffer reproductive problems because of exposure to mutagenic or teratogenic chemicals, or chemicals that give rise to endocrine disorders (ILO 2005).[39] The chemistry we are familiar with will sooner or later have to be replaced by a different one that is more compatible with life, i.e. green or sustainable chemistry.

A different energy model? A different agri-food model? A different chemistry? The dimensions of these changes are colossal. For better or worse, the effects on employment of the transformations that these changes will require, as well as the effects on the means of livelihood of workers and their families, will be enormous.

Natural limitations

These changes, which have already partly been initiated, are not an imaginative proposal; they are technically and economically viable. They are not just a possibility, but an

---

38 This article has been translated from the Spanish. The title was originally "Work and Environment for Sustainable Development – The trade union movement and environmental participation: shaping the change, renewing trade unionism."

39 See also Chapter 2, section 1, "Workers in the workplace and in their communities" by Lene Olsen; Chapter 3, section 3, "Occupational, environmental and public health" by Ivanov, Fedotov and Wehrle-MacDevette; and Chapter 3, section 4, "Chemical risks and hazardous substances" by Tony Musu.

imperative, a constraint derived from natural limitations. Economic development in the medium and long term is not sustained by financial transactions or investments alone, nor is the productivity of the system independent of the natural underlying capital represented by natural resources. The price of petroleum, for example, which will continue to increase as consumption grows and petroleum reserves diminish, can alter not only the economic cycle but the entire growth model of the past decades.

Social development, i.e. human development and well-being – balanced, cohesive and equitable – is not just a question of redistribution and access to goods and services and to decent work, although it is these things as well. It also depends on the greater or lesser abundance of such goods, and their characteristics in any given production system. How can there be more and better jobs for fishermen if the productivity of fishing grounds and catches declines? It will not be possible to give access to electricity to the approximately 1.5 billion poor who are now without it by using an energy system based on large generating centres that depend on non-renewable sources and complex and costly distribution networks.

Ecological footprint

Ecologically, the global system is very inefficient in a world of limited natural resources that are to be distributed among the approximately 6.5 billion inhabitants of the planet and the 9 billion or so who will inhabit it in the second half of the 21st century (UN 2005). For example, if we consider the so-called "ecological footprint" the data are quite revealing: the productive area available per present inhabitant amounts to 1.89 hectare, but average consumption per inhabitant is 2.18 hectares; that is, without having resolved the problems of hunger and poverty in the world, we are occupying or consuming an excess of 0.29 hectares per inhabitant. Consumption per inhabitant is 9.7 hectares by an average North American, 5.6 hectares by an inhabitant of France, and 0.6 hectares by an average Mozambican or Pakistani (Global Footprint Network 2005).

The conclusion is obvious: the production model, energy consumption and diet of developed countries are not generally replicable, simply because the earth does not have sufficient resources. We would need several Planet Earths to make this possible, and we only have one.

Equity and eco-efficiency

We cannot eradicate poverty in the world or achieve social justice by naively imagining that it is possible to extend to all the world's inhabitants the production model that has brought such well-being to developed countries (currently about 20 per cent of humanity). This question is not irrelevant for trade unionism. One of the basic principles of the trade union movement, from its remote origins at the dawn of the Industrial Revolution until today, has been the struggle for social equality. If we also keep in mind that the legitimate basis of trade union action in all countries, including the most developed ones, has been defending the continuation and improvement of workers' occupations, salaries and social protection (i.e. their access to products and services) the solution to the problem of equitable access seems unsolvable. There cannot be social equality without a model change towards sustainability.

Either we change production and consumption patterns, and we manage to hugely increase eco-efficiency to a high enough level to be able to distribute goods and services that ensure the development and well-being of earth's present and future inhabitants, or, inevitably, social conflicts over the appropriation of and access to natural resources will increase.

Socially desirable change

The deterioration of natural resources has the greatest negative effects on the workers and other inhabitants of poor countries, who depend more directly on those resources for their basic needs. In Africa, 70 per cent of the population survives through direct exploitation of natural resources. Rural populations in Asia and Latin America also rely very heavily on direct exploitation of natural resources. Natural resources deterioration seriously affects the chances of survival of people in poor countries.

Adverse environmental impacts have greater negative effects on poor workers and others in the more vulnerable sectors in both the North and South. Drought provoked by climate change will have extreme consequences for rural African communities and workers. The recent drought in the Horn of Africa has brought poverty and hunger to some 11 million people (FAO 2006). But in the North too, poor people and workers are more vulnerable to the effects of natural disasters, which are increasingly occurring with climate change. According to trade unions in the United States, Hurricanes Katrina and Rita put 335 000 employees out of work and the net loss of jobs was some 40 000 (ICFTU/ETUC/TUAC 2005).

The average global temperature increased by 0.6°C during the past century. This has provoked an increase in natural disasters originating in climate change and economic losses likely to amount to over a hundred billion dollars (IPPC 2001). An increase in average temperature of 2.5°C would cause economic losses amounting to between 1.5 and 2 per cent of the world's GNP (Dupressoir and Van Der Hieden 2004). This would be an economic catastrophe, with very serious effects on employment. A change in the model, therefore, is not only an environmental imperative but is socially desirable.[40]

Renewable energy, eradication of poverty and employment

Changing to a sustainable development model is also part of the solution to current human development problems.

In the case of energy, only the immediate and massive expansion of renewable energy will simultaneously address the peak use of petroleum and reduce the CO_2 emissions that are the most important cause of the greenhouse effect, thus at the same time avoiding a very serious economic problem and a major environmental threat. In addition, only massive development of renewable energy, available in situ, will cover the basic energy needs of the earth's inhabitants (many of whom do not have access today to electricity), thus achieving the Millennium Development Goal target for access to basic services.

Such an expansion of renewable energy, sufficient to meet the energy needs of the whole world in 2050, could be achieved by mobilizing just 20 per cent of the investment and resources currently used by the automobile industry. The gains in employment would be quite striking. In Europe, reaching a target of 12 per cent of primary energy through renewable sources by 2010 would create 800 000 new jobs (Riechmann 2001). Meeting the

---

40   Also see Chapter 3, section 1 on "Climate change and energy" by Peter Poschen and Olfa Khazri.

same objective in South Africa would create over 50 000 jobs, redressing the trend of drastic decreases in employment in that country's conventional energy sectors (Hallases 2000).

Green chemistry

Reorganization of the conventional chemical industry (the most polluting of all industries) to green or sustainable chemistry is a necessity not only in order to decrease the toxic pressure on humans and other living beings, which seriously harms health and reproduction, but also to maintain the good services the chemical industry provides to society and the millions of jobs in that industry.

Over 100 000 chemicals are currently produced commercially. Approximately, one-quarter of which have been evaluated for their effects on human health and the environment, leaving some 75 000 chemicals on which no such data is available. This is not to advocate renouncing the benefits of the chemical industry. However, the current industry, which is very dependent on petroleum and its derivatives, must change during this century. A step forward is the new European system known as REACH, which will place new obligations on the industry through a procedure for registration, evaluation and authorization of chemical substances – a system which has met stiff opposition from the industry.[41] But this will still be insufficient. We need to move forward to a different chemistry based on imitation of nature, or biomimesis.

Green chemistry is based on the application of a series of principles by which the use or generation of hazardous substances is reduced or eliminated in the design, manufacture and application of chemical products, using renewable prime matter, making products that are non-toxic and biodegradable and avoiding waste. Numerous chemical products are already being prepared by major companies according to these principles. Green chemistry could greatly expand in coming years, with its products taking the place of polluting chemical substances.

Jobs in decline, emerging jobs

The social repercussions and impact on employment of the necessary transformations in production are of such magnitude that these transformations cannot be effected without a basic consensus in society and among workers. Today employees are an expanding force. There are 2.9 billion workers in the world, some 4.6 billion more than ten years ago. Of these, 900 million work in agriculture, 100 million less than ten years ago; 700 million work in industry, 150 million more; and 1.3 billion are in the service sector, some 350 million more. The prospects for 2015 are for expanded numbers: there will be 3.3 billion million workers, 400 million more than today; employment in agriculture will fall drastically, with 250 million fewer workers, while employment in industry will increase by 150 million. Employment in the service sector will increase by 500 million, with 50 per cent of the total number of workers in this sector.

These figures indicate various trends that need to be considered. First, the work force is expanding and workers represent a huge social potential. Second, the immediate foreseeable scenario is one of major displacement of employment, provoking a diaspora from the agriculture sector even greater than in the past decade, with the migratory rural-urban and South-North consequences that this may imply. Third, the growth of employment

---

41   See Chapter 3, section 4, "Chemical risks and hazardous substances in the workplace" by Tony Musu.

in industry, above all in emerging Asian countries, and the boom in employment in the service sector will be accompanied by a major degradation in employment conditions because of the informal sector and precariousness, as well as the worsening of working conditions, with the low wages and lengthy working days that characterize emerging types of employment.

Global trade unionism faces an extraordinary challenge. On the one hand, it has to adapt its organization and trade union actions to the new realities of labour, making it difficult (although not impossible) to unionize the new informal and precarious employments and to achieve formal employment with rights, i.e. what can be termed a decent job. On the other hand, trade unionism will have to renew and adapt its programme, proposals and actions, directing them towards sustainable development. This means new development, in which some traditional production sectors will run down and become unsustainable, although with a sizable trade union presence, while fresh sectors emerge which have perhaps less trade union presence, but are more sustainable in the long run.

A just transition

All of the foregoing can create social and workplace tensions that need to be understood properly. Let us take, for example, the question of employment. We know that industrial reconversion in favour of sustainable development will generate millions of new jobs, but it could also have adverse effects in sectors that are in decline. We are certain that the new jobs created will be more numerous than those lost. That is the experience of Europe, where environmental policies have given rise to the creation of hundreds of thousands of new jobs. But new jobs are not necessarily created in the same place, or at the same time, as those that are lost.[42] Good management of this environmental reconversion will determine whether it is socially just, is traumatic for workers, meets with the consensus of the labour force or encounters resistance from labour.

Proper management of this process can be achieved through a combination of various factors. One is the attitude and policies of governments and institutions, which need to consider the social and labour-related dimensions of the transition to sustainable development in order to make possible a just transition in social and labour-related terms. Trade unionism will have to come up with new proposals, educate and train its members in environmental matters, and convert itself into a force that is truly committed to sustainable development. Also needed will be the extension of labour rights to the whole labour force, with those rights being widened to include their environmental dimension and the creation of new channels of participation by workers and their representatives, trade unions, and businesses and institutions, all the way from workplaces to the international arena. This will make it possible, in turn, for both public and private employers to recognize such rights and the exercise of these rights in businesses and in sectors.

The trade union movement and civil society

Without effective channels of co-management and labour participation, no consensus on these changes will be possible. Without that consensus, the huge potential for change in the world of workers, which is essential for the needed transformations towards sustainability, will not be able to express itself.

---

42 See Chapter 2, section 1, "Workers in the workplace and in their communities" by Lene Olsen.

Trade unions, after more than a century of growth and with some 200 million organized members, constitute – we should never forget it – the most numerous, experienced and organized part of civil society. In the past century we have achieved a great deal through our organization and our campaigns: we have won the battle to extend social protection and basic labour rights to most countries in the world, including the so-called "welfare state" in some of these countries. We have also managed to extend collective bargaining, with 2.5 million collective agreements signed between business leaders and trade unions which regulate the working conditions of hundreds of millions of workers all over the world. We have succeeded in introducing tripartism, i.e. the joint and balanced participation of governments, employers and trade unions in defining social and labour-related policies in many countries and at the international level, the most outstanding example being the International Labour Organization.

Even modern political democracy has hinged on our struggle, often heroic: the actions of workers and their organizations made an essential contribution to achieving democracy in Spain, Brazil and South Africa, to give only examples from the last quarter of the 20th century.

New trade unions for a new trade unionism

Since the 1992 Rio Conference, trade unions have redoubled their initiatives in favour of sustainable development and of reconciliation between employment and environmental protection. The first global Trade Union Assembly on Labour and the Environment / WILL 2006 was a positive expression of such progress on a global scale. Valuable experiences from five continents were presented and guidelines for future work were agreed.

World trade unionism is undergoing a promising process of unification with the establishment of the International Trade Union Confederation (ITUC) (Box 2.2.1). This process is necessary and encouraging with respect to the challenges of globalization – which is globalization in economic and commercial terms, but not in terms of labour rights and social protection. It is not only a question of moving towards a new International Trade Union Confederation, but also (in the words of the Secretary General of the World Confederation of Labour (WCL), Willy Thys, speaking at the Trade Union Assembly on Labour and the Environment / WILL 2006, of configuring a new trade unionism in which defence of environmental protection and sustainable development will play a substantial role. The programme and statutes of the new confederation follow this line.

From the trade union viewpoint, therefore, major steps are being taken to incorporate workers' views into the environmental agenda. Holding regional trade union conferences on labour and the environment in Latin America and the Caribbean and in Africa in 2006, following the Trade Union Assembly on Labour and the Environment / WILL 2006, is a clear expression of continuing progress in the trade union commitment. For this process to make qualitative progress and achieve practical results, however, some obstacles have to be overcome. The mechanisms of trade union participation in business and in international institutions also need to be extended.

Box 2.2.1

The new International Trade Union Confederation (ITUC)

The International Trade Union Confederation (ITUC) was created on 3 November 2006 through the merger of the International Confederation of Free Trade Unions (ICFTU) and the World Confederation of Labour (WCL).

The ITUC is the main international trade union organization representing the interests of working people worldwide. As of the end of 2006, it had 307 affiliated member organizations in 154 countries and territories, with a total membership of 168 million. The ITUC groups the former affiliates of the ICFTU and WCL, along with trade union organizations which had no previous global affiliation. The ICFTU and the WCL dissolved themselves on 31 October 2006, paving the way for the creation of the ITUC.

The ITUC's primary mission is to promote and defend workers' rights and interests through international cooperation among trade unions, global campaigning, and advocacy within the major global institutions. The Programme Document (adopted at the ITUC Founding Congress in Vienna, Austria, on 1-3 November 2006) sets out the Confederation's overall policy framework, which builds on existing ICFTU and WCL policies. The organization's main areas of activity include: trade union and human rights; economy, society and the workplace; equality and non-discrimination; and international solidarity.

The ITUC adheres to the principles of trade union democracy and independence, as set out in its Constitution. It is governed by four-yearly world congresses, a General Council and an Executive Bureau. The ITUC's chief executive is its General Secretary, Guy Ryder. He is supported by Deputy General Secretaries Mamounata Cisse and Jaap Wienen.

Currently existing ICFTU and WCL regional organizations for Africa, the Americas and Asia-Pacific are expected to be unified by November 2007. The ITUC also co-operates closely with the European Trade Union Confederation (ETUC), including through the ITUC Pan-European Regional Council, to be created in the near future under decisions taken by the ITUC Founding Congress taken by the ITUC Founding Congress.

The ITUC has close relations with the Global Union Federations (GUFs) and the Trade Union Advisory Committee (TUAC) to the OECD, working together through the Global Unions Council. It has observer status at the United Nations Economic and Social Council and works closely with the International Labour Organization (ILO). It maintains contacts with several other UN specialized agencies. Along with its regional organizations and their sub-offices, the ITUC has offices in Amman (Jordan), Geneva, Moscow, New York, Sarajevo (Bosnia and Herzegovina), Vilnius (Lithuania) and Washington, DC. The main areas outlined in the IUTC's programme are:

- Changing globalization;
- The challenge of multinational business;
- Defending and promoting trade union rights;
- Fighting discrimination, achieving equality;
- Ending child labour;
- A decent future for young workers;
- Making workplaces healthy and safe;
- The ILO: global reference point;
- Peace, security and the United Nations;
- Organize!;
- The new internationalism.

ITUC membership includes all the membership of ICFTU and WCL

Obstacles to worker participation in environmental activities

The main obstacles to participation in environmental activities by workers are lack of understanding by governments and opposition by business.

Too often, governments do not appear to understand well what trade unions can bring to environmental policy. In part, this happens because the environmental and labour agendas are different, and most governments do not apply an integrated sustainable development policy. Thus ministers of environment do not understand why they should be concerned about workers, while labour ministers do not understand why they should be concerned about the environment. As a result, environmental negotiations do not consider the social and labour-related effects of environmental policies, although they do consider the economic ones, while in social and labour-related negotiations environmental aspects are usually never considered.

However, this is changing, as shown by several examples. In Germany energy policies for reducing CO_2 emissions have involved trade unions, and an Alliance for Work and the Environment has been established to promote such policies and direct them towards the creation of employment, accompanied by an investment of US$1.8 billion (Box 3.1.4). In Spain Sectoral Round Tables on Social Dialogue have been set up to implement the Kyoto Protocol in industrial sectors, with the participation of the Government, trade unions and business organizations. In Argentina the Government has adopted a programme on work and the environment (Box 2.2.2). In Brazil the Ministries of Environment and Labour are negotiating the adoption of a similar programme.

The main obstacles to environmental participation by workers originate in businesses, which habitually resist any extension of labour and trade union rights at the workplace and refuse to account for their actions to workers' representatives.

Many polluting businesses assume that workers and trade unions share their anti-environmental biases. They even encourage labour mobilization against increasing demands by governments, and by society in general, for greater environmental responsibility, while at the same time threatening us with loss of employment. Only then do they remember that workers are a concerned party in environmental policies, when we have not been given a single opportunity to anticipate the problems so as to avoid them. Such occasions do not provide an opening for worker participation, but simply use workers as a sort of social shield to escape from emerging environmental requirements.

Part of the difficulty of ensuring workers' participation in decision-making on environmental issues arises from the lack of workers' environmental rights. Because of the out-of-phase nature of the historical configuration of workers' rights, their environmental rights are not dealt with in current legislation. The norms and standards of labour laws, which have a long tradition, were established in times when there was no environmental agenda. When, in the past few decades, the norms and standards that make up environmental law were developed, this took place without any consideration of labour rights.

Nevertheless, in numerous areas we have made advances regarding participation, ranging from the international arena to workplaces.

Box 2.2.2

Argentina: Framework Environmental Agreement between the Government and the CGTRA[43]

In Argentina the General Confederation of Labour (Confederación General de Trabajo – CGT) has a framework agreement on environment with the Government.

The incorporation of environmental clauses in collective agreements and the participation of workers in policy process were necessary to achieve sustainable development, which is defined as encompassing better working conditions, better job opportunities, an expansion of employment and strict compliance with ILO conventions. The objective of the framework agreement is to:

- Create a new alliance on labour and the environment;
- Involve the labour movement in the debate on, and implementation and follow-up of national environmental policies;
- Build a bipartite co-ordination agency between government and unions on the environment;
- Open institutional spaces in the environmental agenda to ensure full participation by workers in addressing each issue (clean production, climate change, alternative energies, Mercosur, hazardous substances, forests, desertification, rural environment);
- Train environmental delegates in each sector of activity;
- Define characteristics and methodologies for a just transition;
- Obtain tools to include environmental clauses in the collective agreements.

To this end, the CGT formulated a national environmental agenda, signed an agreement establishing a co-ordinating committee with the Ministries of Health, Labour and Environment, worked with other international workers' organizations, and disseminated information through educational material and workshops. The union seeks workers' participation in policy development, promoting the inclusion of environmental provisions in trade unions' collective agreements and the training of union officers.

The agreement aims to involve workers and trade unions in debating, implementing and monitoring national environmental policies by making them aware of and committed to labour and environmental policies. Moreover, the agreement intends to create an agency with bipartite co-ordination between the Government and trade unions to make an institutional space in the environmental agenda to guarantee workers' participation. The agreement also proposes creating environmental delegates in each sector of activity.

Future activities include:

- Training for environmental delegates;
- Creation of a political and technical document to be presented to the National Executive, including mechanisms for just transition;
- Implementation of good practices by workers in each sector of activity, to allow the creation of new jobs and better wages.

---

43 Based on the case study presented by Abel Frutos, representing the Confederación General de Trabajo – CGT, at the Trade Union Assembly on Labour and the Environment / WILL 2006.

The international front

The international front is not the least important of these areas. In a globalized world such as ours, with global problems like climate change or ocean pollution, the international front is the area in which the decisions that most affect workers and coming generations are made. That is why trade union participation on the international front is of such vital importance.

Trade unions have therefore been increasingly active with respect to the environmental agenda of the United Nations, stimulated and co-ordinated by the International Confederation of Free Trade Unions (ICFTU) and the Trade Union Advisory Council (TUAC) to the OECD. If trade union participants at the 1992 Rio Conference could be counted on the fingers of both hands, their participation at the 2002 Johannesburg Summit they could be counted in the hundreds. Some international agreements and processes have had a trade union presence from the outset, e.g. the Framework Convention on Climate Change (UNFCCC), the Kyoto Protocol, the Stockholm Convention on Persistent Organic Chemicals (POPs) and the Strategic Approach to International Chemicals Management (SAICM) negotiations on chemicals management.[44] We always participate actively in the annual sessions of the UN Commission on Sustainable Development.

A new and encouraging phase for trade unions opened with the first global Trade Union Assembly on Labour and the Environment / WILL 2006. The meeting had a very wide and fully representative trade union presence. The Final Resolution adopted by the trade union representatives established the basic guidelines for trade union action on environmental matters, while the launching of a programme of activities on work and the environment (including capacity-building, training, and dissemination of practical experience) initiated a new and auspicious chapter for trade unions, and indeed also for UNEP, which can only fully fulfil its mandate to protect the environment if it has the backing of all of society and of workers, who are represented by trade unions and are a substantial part of society.

The World Health Organization, for its part, has for some time been laying great stress on the close links between the deterioration of environmental conditions and human health: 25 per cent of illnesses in the world have environmental causes, giving rise to some 13 million deaths a year (WHO 2006). A number of these deaths occur in or because of workplaces. Not only does WHO aim to reduce deaths and illnesses originating at the workplace because of unhealthy, unsafe or unsustainable production methods. It also works to achieve healthy environments for workers and communities. Concerning that objective, WHO and the trade union movement are strategic allies. To fully develop the potential of this alliance with specific work programmes would represent a considerable advance in simultaneously improving occupational health, public health and environmental health.[45]

The International Labour Organization (ILO) has three essential contributions to make to this process:

❑ Tripartism, without which it would be difficult to bring the influence of trade unions to bear on policies that affect workers, including environmental policies;

---

44 See Chapter 3, section 4,"Chemical risks and hazardous substances in the workplace" by Tony Musu.
45 See Chapter 3, section 3, "Occupational, environmental and public health" by Ivan D. Ivanov, Igor Fedetov and Monica Wehrele-MacDevette.

- ❑ The content of ILO agreements, which range all the way from the specific right to health at the workplace to the rights of trade union freedom and collective bargaining – rights without which workers could not exercise their other rights, and without which labour participation could not exist;
- ❑ The understanding that to have a decent job is a precondition for eradicating poverty and is part of the very content of sustainable development.

The commitment of UNEP, ILO and WHO to collaborate with trade unions in developing the environmental agenda will provide an opportunity to fully extend this agenda to the world of labour.

The regional front

Several components of the regional front should not be overlooked, as it is at the regional or sub-regional level that modern approaches to the integration of markets and policies are worked out, and therefore, decision-making that affects workers and others and the environment. Reference is made not only to the European Union, configured as it is like a regional multi-state proto-State, but also to processes such as the Latin American Common Market of the South (Mercosur) or the New Partnership for Africa's Development (NEPAD). Opportunities for trade union participation in regional environmental agendas vary greatly. While in Europe we are assured of active participation through the European Trade Union Confederation (ETUC), thanks to a favourable conjunction of factors (a strong trade union movement, advanced European environmental policies, available areas of participation), in other regional processes this is still an unresolved issue. However, conditions for progress in matters of work and environment in the Mercosur area are quite favourable.[46]

National frameworks

Given countries' political and juridical configuration and the type of multilateral agreements binding them in environmental matters, the country level continues to be key to the adoption of policies, and therefore also to participation. Depending on how labour laws and environmental policies are articulated, they provide frameworks that are favourable or unfavourable to environmental participation by trade unions. The establishment of national sustainable development committees in many countries following the 1992 Rio Conference on Environment and Development, with participation by trade union organizations, has been a decisive stimulus for the development of trade union participation at country level. That level is also the one at which we have the most accumulated experience.

It is national governments that must take action on this issue. However, they will not do so unless trade unions persistently push them in that direction. Recognition of the right to environmental participation by trade unions in national policy-making by trade unions is quite well accepted in the EU Member States and in some other countries, such as Brazil, but it is very far from being generally recognized, especially in developing countries.

---

46 The countries which are full members of Mercusor are Argentina, Brazil, Paraguay, Uruguay and Venezuela. The associate members are Bolivia, Chile, Colombia, Ecuador and Peru. Mexico has observer status and is in the process of becoming an associate member.

Workplaces

The workplace is the area where labour relations take effect. It is the proper and authentic framework for trade union action. It is here that workers build support among themselves and in their communities. It is also where health risks occur and activities are carried out that impact the workplace surroundings.[47] Controlling the environmental impacts of businesses' activities is not contrary to workers' interests. If a business acts irresponsibly in environmental matters, workers may lose their jobs. Toxic substances that harm their health at work also pollute their community; and, as citizens, the positive or negative global effects of a particular production activity are not a matter of indifference to any of us.

Workers and their representatives could have a key function on the path towards greater environmental responsibility at the workplace: collaborating in applying best practices to save water and energy and minimize waste; contributing to meeting environmental rules, especially for discharges and emissions that pollute water and the atmosphere; and encouraging technological advances and the development of research in favour of technologies and products that are environment-friendly. There are numerous examples of the useful function performed by workers' trade union representatives in matters of health, as well as a growing and positive experience of labour and trade union activities that benefit the environment at the workplace.

Environmental delegates

The occupational safety delegate elected by workers in industries has been an extraordinary tool for defending workers' health and safety and a healthy working environment. These delegates may also work on environmental matters, but they do not do so as a general rule, as they lack specific entitlement to take action on environmental issues.

If environmental delegates' mandates and powers were extended, or if these delegates were elected in larger enterprises (or in enterprises with greater environmental impact), it would be possible to have more widespread environmental activities in workplaces. At present such a right is not envisaged in national legislation, even in the EU, although recognition of such rights is beginning to be conceded in some large enterprises, and in sectoral collective agreements and voluntary regional accords.

In Spain, for example, there are regions such as Navarre where the environmental delegate is designated by tripartite agreement. The environmental delegate may visit businesses to help workers exercise their rights to be informed, and to contribute to reducing or eliminating environmental impacts at their workplaces. Several examples include collective agreements such as the General Chemical Industry Convention, which affects all workers in the sector, recognition of the right to nominate environmental delegates in enterprises; and company agreements which recognize such a delegate, as at the Michelin Company. In many other Spanish collective agreements occupational safety delegates have been given wider rights and responsibilities, also recognizing their right to information and action in environmental matters.

---

47   See, in particular, Chapters 1, "Labour and the Environment: A Natural Synergy" by Sophie De Coninck and Hilary French; Chapter 2, section 1, "Workers in the Workplace and in their Communities" by Lene Olsen; Chapter 3, section 3, "Occupational, environmental and public health" by Ivan D. Ivanov, Igor Fedetov and Monica Wehrele-MacDevette; and Chapter 3, section 4, "Chemical risks and hazardous substances in the workplace" by Tony Musu.

Corporate social responsibility

The prolific adoption of Corporate Social Responsibility (CSR) principles by numerous enterprises in recent years could be a useful area for the exercise of these rights, provided that they are genuine processes and not merely public relations exercises, as often happens. Even more useful would be the adoption of CSR by multinational companies, provided that this is carried out with genuine social and environmental responsibility criteria.

Participation in such processes would enable the eradication of labour-related and environmentally aggressive actions in third countries and the defence of decent work standards and health and safety protection measures at the workplace and with respect to the environment (i.e. measures that would be more advanced than those currently recognized in each individual country's legislation). International trade union federations have already signed some 40 agreements with various multinational companies, mostly based in Europe. The results, including those related to the environment, need to be evaluated and appropriate lessons drawn for future guidance.

Alliances

Intergovernmental bodies, national governments, business organizations and companies are our natural interlocutors. We seek and will continue to seek agreements with each of them, through social dialogue:

❑ To promote production transformations for the benefit of sustainable development;
❑ To disseminate new technologies that are environment-friendly;
❑ To encourage the development of emerging and sustainable sectors;
❑ To create decent and sustainable employment in such sectors;
❑ To foresee possible adverse problems that might occur in sectors in decline, and to find possible solutions and just transition mechanisms.

If governments and enterprises are our interlocutors, our allies are the whole of organized civil society: scientists, with whom we share the path of technological innovation on the way to a more efficient production system and a less material-minded economy; agriculture organizations, with which we need to find joint solutions to change the agro-food model; indigenous communities; women, whose struggle for equality at the workplace and for reproductive health is also our struggle; youth (e.g. younger workers and trade unionists); consumers, with whom we have to learn how to change both production and consumption patterns; and environmental NGOs, which are showing an ever-increasing social commitment to a future fruitful convergence.

Alliances are never easy. The positions of each side are not always automatically the same - not even among workers, who always have common interests. But we also know that framing proposals jointly is a powerful tool that should help such proposals to succeed, and that recognition by civil society of the world of labour's function and potential to change society towards a sustainable outlook will broaden the path of participation. It all remains to be done. If a socially more just and environmentally more stable world is possible, we must achieve it together (Box 2.2.3).

It is up to the trade union movement to follow its path of renewal. In the phase now beginning, in which the international trade union unity process coincides with the impulse given by the environmental agenda to the trade union agenda, the commitment assumed by Guy Ryder, Secretary General of ICFTU, during the Trade Union Assembly on Labour and the Environment / WILL 2006 in favour of integrating the environmental dimension of sustainable development into trade union actions (and including the environment in collective bargaining) clearly indicates the direction of the process on which we have embarked.

Box 2.2.3

Namibia: A local union takes on a multinational corporation[48]

A case study presented at the Trade Union Assembly on Labour and the Environment/WILL 2006 by a representative of the International Textile, Garment and Leather Workers' Federation (ITGLWF) illustrates the difficult issues that can arise following the implementation of a free trade agreement. This study focuses on corporate social responsibility, OHS and environment.

There was theoretical support in Namibia for reliance on free trade agreements, as the country did not have an industrial base. Nevertheless, the reality was largely detrimental for Namibian workers and other citizens, who received low wages and were subject to unfair labour conditions, poor occupational safety and health, and negative environmental consequences.

The main objectives of union activities were to make the Malaysian-owned Ramatex company comply with international standards and national laws, and to bring about change and improvements at the local factory level. This involved participation by various stakeholders, including retailers.

The case

The Ramatex garment factory opened in Namibia under the African Growth and Opportunity Act (AGOA).[49] However, it did not install waste water disposal technology as planned, resulting in contamination of the water supply of Windhoek, Namibia's capital. The case raised the issues of the need for clear environmental and occupational standards, in order to protect workers' rights, and the need for corporate and regulatory transparency.

On the basis of AGOA rules, to attract Ramatex to Namibia the Government offered huge concessions including the investment of over N$100 million in public funds to build infrastructure for the company, a 99-year tax exemption, and subsidized water and electricity. From the outset, it was apparent that the company was unwilling to abide by national laws and regulations. The Government presented it with an ultimatum to register with the Ministry of Labour, as well as to make legally required contributions to social security and compensation funds.

A labour dispute which occurred soon after the company began operations led to an agreement with the Namibian Food and Allied Workers' Union (NAFAU). It appeared that significant progress was being made, and that Ramatex would opt for social dialogue rather than industrial conflict. Nevertheless, a series of disputes over the course of two years, arising from the company's labour practices, demonstrated that Ramatex paid no heed to national or international labour laws. The Government had justified its incentive package on the grounds that Ramatex would create thousands of new jobs, helping to alleviate the country's massive unemployment problem.

---

48   Based on the case study presented by Silvana Cappuccio, representing the International Textile, Garment and Leather Workers' Federation (ITGLWF), at the Trade Union Assembly on Labour and the Environment / WILL 2006.

49   The AGOA was signed into law on 18 May 2000, as Title 1 of The Trade and Development Act of 2000, "to offer tangible incentives for African countries to continue their efforts to open their economies and build free markets" (www.agoa.gov).

Box 2.2.3 (...cont'd)

In reality, while some 8 000 jobs were created, nearly one-quarter were held by migrant workers from Asia. The company claimed that these workers had been brought in as trainers, but this was manifestly untrue. Clearly it was bringing in low-paid workers who (it believed) were unlikely to protest over poor conditions in view of their vulnerability.

Health and safety was a major source of contention at the Ramatex factory, with most workers reporting that they had not been supplied with necessary protective equipment. In July 2002, a few months after Ramatex began its operations in Namibia, a government investigation into employee's claims of health problems revealed that they suffered from respiratory diseases, chest problems and skin rashes.

Another study, led by a South African NGO, revealed that work-related accidents occurred on a daily basis. Foreign workers complained about squalid living and working conditions, as well as lack of hygiene in the canteen where food was prepared. For a time, migrant workers refused to eat food prepared there.

There was also great concern locally that the factory had not installed the technology to dispose of its waste water, which was contaminated with toxins from washing and dyeing of fabrics. City officials were denied access to the plant to inspect the facilities. The press reported there were signs that the city's underground water sources were contaminated by toxins from "wet processing" at the plant.

The ITGLWF made retailers sourcing from Ramatex aware of the company's appalling labour practices and asked them to take action to ensure that it abided by international labour standards. With a catalogue of evidence revealing the reasons for growing discontent among the workforce, the ITGLWF called upon all Ramatex buyers to bring pressure on the company. The aim was to put in place a corrective action programme to address poor labour practices and abuses of workers' rights. Best practice in the sector indicated that this would be best achieved with full involvement of the trade union concerned through collective bargaining.

Lessons learnt

This case is a concrete example of how existing international trade agreements dramatically impact environmental and social conditions. The ITGLWF supported the union in demanding that Ramatex respect national labour and immigration laws, that it begin negotiating in good faith a comprehensive collective agreement with the union, and that it ensure the rights all workers, including protecting migrants without discrimination.

In conclusion, the primacy given to free trade agreements in the international trade agenda – above environmental and social considerations – was detrimental to African development.

References

- Confederación Sindical de Comisiones Obreras (CCOO) and Instituto Sindical de Trabajo, Ambiente y Salud (ISTAS) (Spain) (2004). De Río a Johanesbourgo. Una década de experiencias sindicales por el medio ambiente.

- Dupressoir, Sophie and Sebastián Van Der Hieden (2004). Climate Change. Avenues for Trade Union Action. European Trade Union Confederation (ETUC) (www.etuc.org/a/957).

- EUTC (European Trade Union Confederation) (2005). Review of the EU Sustainable Development Strategy (Declaration adopted by the ETUC Executive Committee, 14-15 June) (www.etuc.org/a/1417).

- FAO (Food and Agriculture Organization of the United Nations) (2006). Millions of people are on the brink of starvation in the Horn of Africa (FAO Newsroom, 6 January) (www.fao.org/newsroom/eS/news/2006/1000206/index.html).

- Global Footprint Network (2005). 2005 National Footprint Accounts (www.footprintnetwork.org/gfn_sub.php?content=footprint_hectares).

- Hallases, David (2000). Towards a Civil Society Review of South African Energy Policy and Implementation. Sustainable Energy and Climate Change Power. Johannesburg.

- ICFTU (International Confederation of Free Trade Unions) (2004). Final Resolution: Globalization, Decent Work and Sustainable Development. 18th World Congress, Miyazaki (Japan), 5-10 December (www.ilo.org/public/english/fairglobalization/download/events/5_3_198_icftu1.pdf).

- ICFTU/ETUC/TUAC (International Confederation of Free Trade Unions/European Trade Union Confederation/Trade Union Advisory Committee (TUAC) to the OECD) (2005). Preventing Disruption and Enhancing Community Cohesion Social and Employment Transition for Climate.

- ILO (International Labour Organization) (2005). Decent Work – Safe Work, ILO Introductory Report to the XVIIth World Congress on Safety and Health at Work (www.ilo.org/public/english/protection/safework/wdcongrs17/intrep.pdf).

— (2006). LABORSTA (database on labour statistics operated by the ILO Bureau of Statistics) (http://laborsta.ilo.org).

- IPPC (Intergovernmental Panel on Climate Change) (2001). Third Assessment Report – Climate Change 2001 (The Scientific Basis; Impacts, Adaptation and Vulnerability; Mitigation; Synthesis Report) (www.grida.no/climate/ipcc_tar). These reports may be downloaded from the IPPC website in Arabic, Chinese, English, French, Russian and Spanish. Unofficial translations into Danish, Japanese and German may also be downloaded from this site (www.grida.no/climate/ipcc_tar).

— (1996). Revised 1996 IPCC Guidelines for National Greenhouse Gas Inventories. The Reporting Instructions (Volume I) (www.ipcc-nggip.iges.or.jp/public/gl/invs4.htm).

- ISTAS (Instituto Sindical de Trabajo, Ambiente y Salud) (Spain) (2004). Guía para la intervención: La prevención del riesgo químico en el lugar de trabajo.

- (2005). Cambio climático: efectos sobre los sectores productivos.

- Nieto Sainz, Joaquín (2005). Cambio Climático y protocolo de Kioto: efectos sobre el empleo, la salud y el medio ambiente. Información Comercial Española (ICE). May.

References (...cont'd)

- Riechmann, Jorge (2001). Efectos sobre el empleo de la lucha contra el cambio climática. Daphnia 25, July. Based on the report Energy Innovations from the Union of Concerned Scientists (www.ucsusa.org/clean_energy/renewable_energy_basics/energy-innovations-a-prosperous-path-to-a-clean-environment.html).

- TUSDAC (Trade Union Sustainable Development Advisory Committee) (2005). A Fair and Just Transition. Research report for Greening the Workplace (www.sustainlabour.org/documents/programmes/TUSDAC_Greening_the_Workplace_EN.pdf).

- UN (United Nations News Services) (2005). World population to reach 9.1 billion in 2050 (News Centre, 24 February) (www.un.org/apps/news/story.asp?NewsID=13451&Cr=population&Cr1).

- WHO (World Health Organization) (2006). Preventing Disease through Healthy Environments – Towards an Estimate of the Environmental Burden of Disease (www.who.int/quantifying_ehimpacts/publications/preventingdisease/en/index.html)

3. Labour and the Environment: Common Perspectives on Specific Issues

Peter Poschen and *Olfa Khazri*, *Sustainable Development Group, Policy Integration Department, International Labour Organization*

© Cordeiro / UNEP

Charcoal burners, Brazil: *Because poor people have limited financial resources, they depend on the environment for their basic needs, such as water, food, shelter. When environmental degradation occurs, the capacity of poor people to make decisions that contribute to their well-being is undermined. Workers are often the very first victims of environmental degradation.*

3.1. Climate change and energy

Climate change and energy have both been high on the development agenda, as the world approaches what has been variously referred to as the "climax of humanity"[50] or the "bottleneck"[51] that will be reached around the year 2050. Until then the world population will continue to grow. At the same time, according to some projections, poverty should have been eradicated by 2050, while quality of life is maintained and the socio-economic pathways which would irreversibly damage the environment (i.e. the natural systems that support life on earth) are avoided. Economic growth is needed, but it has to be based on sustainable patterns of production and consumption.

How are energy and fossil fuels central to growth? To what extent does this pose a dilemma between short-term growth and long-term quality of life and sustainability? Much of the dilemma could be resolved by overcoming the separation of agendas and differences in time scales which characterize the debate and decision-making. Even closely related policy areas like energy security, land use and climate change are not integrated. Impacts on employment, income and poverty are likely to be significant. These impacts should be a key element in the search for sustainable development, but social concerns are still too absent from the debate.

Trade unions have already played an active and positive role in this debate and in the implementation of practical steps (e.g. at the 14th session of the UN Commission on Sustainable Development in May 2006) (UNCSD 2006). The trade union contribution will be vital in order to put social concerns on the agenda, and to promote and accelerate steps towards the sustainable production and consumption patterns that humankind and the earth need.

Patterns of growth, the technologies used to achieve this growth, distribution of the wealth generated, and environmental impacts are all closely inter-related. Economic, social and environmental factors and outcomes are therefore intimately linked and need to be addressed by coherent policies. Such policies, by avoiding trade-offs between economic, environmental and social objectives, and by seizing the opportunity to address different policy objectives simultaneously, would promote more and earlier steps towards the reconciliation of conflicting issues. This chapter explores the inter-relations between growth, energy and climate change and their social dimensions. It analyzes the likelihood of scenarios for future policies, and identifies important gaps in knowledge and decision-making which trade unions are well-placed to help address.

---

50 "After several centuries of faster-than-exponential growth, the world's population is stabilizing. Judging from current trends, it will plateau at around nine billion people toward the middle of this century. Meanwhile extreme poverty is receding both as a percentage of population and in absolute numbers. If China and India continue to follow in the economic footsteps of Japan and South Korea, by 2050 the average Chinese will be as rich as the average Swiss is today; the average Indian, as rich as today's Israeli. As humanity grows in size and wealth, however, it increasingly presses against the limits of the planet. Already we pump out carbon dioxide three times as fast as the oceans and land can absorb it; midcentury is when climatologists think global warming will really begin to bite. At the rate things are going, the world's forests and fisheries will be exhausted even sooner." Excerpted from editorial "The Climax of Humanity" in Scientific American (Musser 2005).

51 The bottleneck is what I believe humanity's in right now. We all, or most all, realize that humanity has pushed its population growth pretty close to the limit. We really are at risk of using up natural resources and developing shortages in them that will be extremely difficult to overcome, and yet we have this bright prospect down the line that humanity is not going to keep on growing much more in population, that it is likely, if we can use the United Nations' projections at this stage, to top out at perhaps nine to ten billion, fifty percent more people than exist today, and then begin to decline." Excerpted from an interview with the scientist Edward O. Wilson (2004).

A driving force: energy and economic growth

Economic growth is indispensable to meet the material needs of the world's growing population, and to lift out of poverty the more than half the people on earth who survive on less than US$2/day (ILO 2006,World Bank 2005). This situation is aggravated by uneven distribution of the wealth generated by economic growth. With a disproportionately small share going to the poorest groups, much higher levels of growth are needed if poverty is to be overcome.

Several independently obtained projections agree that world gross domestic product (GDP) in 2030 should be 240 per cent of that in 2000 (in real terms, i.e. adjusted for purchasing power parity) (Kok and De Coninck 2004). This would require annual growth rates of more than 3 per cent. If historical experience is anything to go by, such growth rates would, in turn, require massive amounts of energy. Economic growth and energy use have been closely correlated. Energy consumption is therefore expected to continue to increase steadily, as shown in Figure 3.1.1. But energy not only powers economic growth.

Figure 3.1.1

World marketed energy consumption by region, 1970-2025
Quadrillion Btu [52]

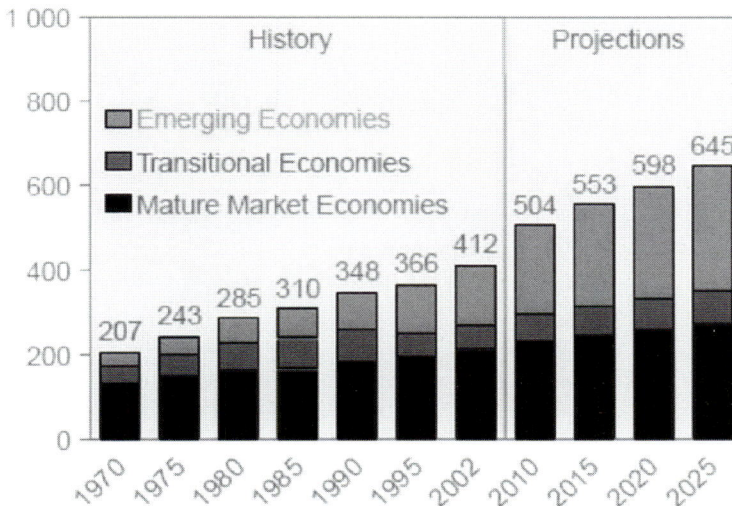

Source: Energy Information Administration (EIA) 2005.

Energy use and climate change

Because of the energy sources and technology used, energy consumption also drives climate change. In 2001 around 80 per cent of all energy was supplied by fossil fuels,

---

52 "The British thermal unit (BTU or Btu) is a unit of energy used in North America. It is also still occasionally encountered in the United Kingdom, in the context of older heating and cooling systems. In most other areas, it has been replaced by the SI unit of energy, the joule (J). In the United States, the term ... is used to describe the heat value (energy content) of fuels, and also to describe the power of heating and cooling systems, such as furnaces, stoves, barbecue grills, and air conditioners. When used as a unit of power, BTU per hour is understood, though this is often confusingly abbreviated to just BTU." Excerpted from http://en.wikipedia.org/wiki/Btu.

primarily coal, oil and natural gas (EIA 2005). Energy is generated by burning these fuels. This releases carbon dioxide, the most important cause of the greenhouse effect.

A number of gases reduce the ability of the earth's atmosphere to return part of the energy received from the sun back to space. More energy is retained and, over time, this leads to an overall rise in temperatures, i.e. global warming. The main gases responsible for the greenhouse effect are (Munasinghe and Swart 2005):

❑ Carbon dioxide (CO2) (approximately 60 per cent of positive radiative forcing);[53]
❑ Methane (CH4) (20 per cent);
❑ Nitrous oxide (NO2) (6 per cent);
❑ Hydrofluorocarbons (HFCs) (14 per cent).

Emissions of HFCs have been greatly reduced since they were banned because they destroy the ozone layer, which protects the earth against ultraviolet radiation from the sun. These substances are long-lived, however, and will continue to contribute to global warming for hundreds or even thousands of years.[54]

Global warming is produced above all by CO_2 in the atmosphere. Fully three-quarters of CO_2 emissions are released through the burning of fossil fuels. The remaining 25 per cent comes mostly from land use change, particularly the destruction and conversion of forests. Both of these types of emissions are the result of human activity (Munasinghe and Swart 2005).

Prior to the Industrial Revolution, the atmospheric concentration of CO_2 was 280 ppm (parts per million). Today it is equal to 367 ppm or more,[55] the highest concentration in 420 000 years. Emissions from human activities are thought to release 6 billion tonnes of CO_2 per year to the atmosphere. This is having extremely serious consequences.

Direct impacts of climate change

The danger of human induced climate change was recognized as early as 1896 by the Swedish chemist Svante Arrhenius (1859-1927). Understanding of the process, its causes and its likely impacts was of course limited. This understanding has improved very significantly, particularly over the last five to ten years. The Intergovernmental Panel on Climate Change (IPCC) concluded in its Third (and most recent) Assessment Report that "there is new and stronger evidence that most of the warming observed over the last

---

53 "As a general concept, the term radiative forcing in climate science means any change in the radiation (heat) entering or leaving the climate system. It can be due to changes in sunlight arriving, or to differing amounts of radiatively active gases…A positive forcing tends to warm the system while a negative forcing tends to cool it." Excerpted from http://en.wikipedia.org/wiki/Radiative_forcing.

54 HFCs are high global warming potential (GWP) gases. "Hydrofluorocarbons (HFCs), perfluorocarbons (PFCs), and sulphur hexafluoride (SF$_6$) are potent greenhouse gases, and some persist in the environment for thousands of years. These gases, referred to as high global warming potential gases (high GWPs), are from 140-23,900 times more potent than CO_2 in terms of their capabilities to trap heat in the atmosphere over a 100-year period. Also, because they remain in the atmosphere almost indefinitely, concentrations of these gases will increase as long as emissions continue." Excerpted from the United States Environmental Protection Agency (US EPA) High GWP Gases web page (www.epa.gov/highgwp/).

55 367 ppm is the figure for atmospheric concentration of CO_2 agreed by the IPCC in its Third Assessment Report (IPCC 2001). In March 2006 the World Meteorological Organization (WMO) reported that the global average atmospheric concentration of CO_2 in 2004 was 377.1 ppm, representing an increase during that year of 1.8 ppm (WMO 2006). Also in 2006, the United States National Oceanic and Atmospheric Administration (NOAA) reported that the average atmospheric concentration of CO_2 in 2005 reached 381 ppm, representing an increase of 2.6 ppm since 2004 (Pearce 2006). For atmospheric CO_2 concentrations since 1958, derived from in situ air samples collected at NOAA's Mauna Loa Observatory in Hawaii, see http://news.mongabay.com/2006/0313-co2.html.

50 years is attributable to human activities. Human influence will continue to change atmospheric composition throughout the 21st century" (IPCC 2001).[56]

The consensus among the overwhelming majority of scientists today includes the following (IPCC 2001, Munasinghe and Swart 2005):

❑ The global mean surface temperature increased by 0.6±0.2°C over the 20th century;
❑ Global mean sea level increased at an average annual rate of 1 to 2 mm during the 20th century, as the heat content of oceans rose (but not yet because of melting ice caps);
❑ Most warming during the last 50 years is the result of human activity;
❑ Extreme wetness and drought are being experienced more often, particularly in parts of Asia and Africa;
❑ Continental precipitation is likely to have increased by 5 to 10 per cent over the 20th century in the northern hemisphere, although it decreased in some regions (e.g. north and west Africa and parts of the Mediterranean region);
❑ El Niño events have become more frequent, persistent and intense during the last 20 to 30 years, compared to the previous 100 years; [57]
❑ In all scenarios, CO_2 is the most important factor;
❑ All scenarios predict rising temperatures for hundreds and rising sea levels for thousands of years, even if emissions of greenhouse gases were reduced to the levels of the year 2000.

Climate change is real, but it is a process that gathers momentum slowly. In particular, the oceans act as a buffer. Temperature and sea-level rises, as well as other manifestations of climate change, therefore only occur much later than the emissions that triggered them (Figure 3.1.2). These changes are expected to happen gradually, building a sense of urgency very slowly. Nevertheless, stabilization of atmospheric concentrations of CO_2 at any level will require an eventual reduction of global net emissions to a small fraction of the current level. After atmospheric concentrations of CO_2 and other greenhouse gases have been stabilized, surface air temperature is projected to continue to rise by a few tenths of a degree per century for a century or more, while sea-level rises are projected to continue for many centuries (IPCC 2001). Projections for the year 2100, based on a likely combination of growth and energy use, show a rise in average temperatures of 1.4 to 5.8°C and a sea-level rise of 9 to 88 cm (Houghton et al. 2001).

Extreme weather events such as floods, droughts, and heat or cold waves are believed to be more damaging than average temperature changes or rises in sea levels, at least in the foreseeable future. Long-term projections are obviously difficult to make. It is also not known whether changes will be continuous, gradual and reversible, or whether there could be abrupt changes. This could alter the outlook drastically, e.g. for sea-level rises. There is enough water in the world's ice sheets to cause sea levels to rise by 70 metres. With present knowledge, large-scale, abrupt and irreversible changes are unlikely until 2100. But it should be noted that some recent studies have called this into question.

---

56   The Fourth IPCC Assessment Report will be completed in 2007 (www.ippc.ch).
57   The El Niño phenomenon occurs every few years in the Pacific Ocean. A mass of warm water, moving from west to east, rises as it travels and produces very high tides along the western coast of South America. "The 1997-98 El Niño event affected virtually every [global] region. Eastern Africa suffered drought and unusually high rainfall; Southeast Asia and North America, abnormally warm periods; South Asia, drought; Latin America and the Caribbean, unusually high rainfall and drought; and the Pacific Islands unusually high rainfall...More than 110 million people were affected and more than 6 million people were displaced as community infrastructures, including housing, food storage, transport and communications, were lost during storms. Direct economic losses exceeded US$34 billion." Excerpted from UNEP 2002 ("GEO-3"), p. 272. Also see, among other sources, http://en.wikipedia.org/wiki/El_Nino; Rory Carroll, "Trouble at the Top", 3 January 2007 (http://environment.guardian.co.uk).

Figure 3.1.2

CO₂ concentration, temperature and sea level continue to rise long after emissions are reduced

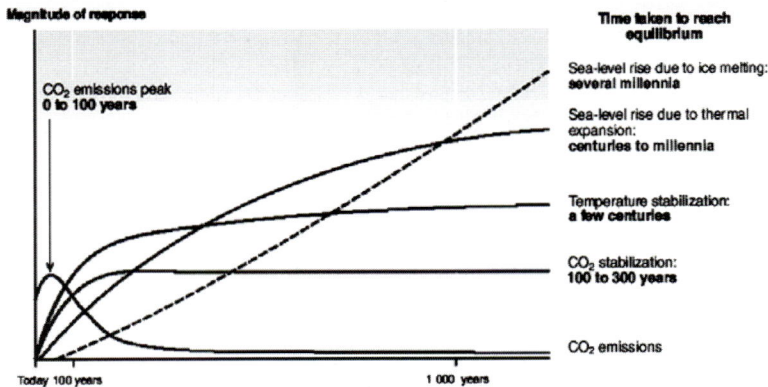

Source: IPCC 2001.

Socio-economic impacts of climate change

The magnitude and proportions of impacts on natural systems and people – and the time frame in which these impacts occur – will depend on their vulnerability and on the course of action chosen with respect to economic growth and energy.

Impacts will differ substantially across regions, and across populations within regions. There is broad agreement on two findings (IPCC 2001, Munasinghe and Swart 2005):

❑ Developing countries are more vulnerable than industrialized ones. They will suffer higher impacts and they have less capacity to adapt;

❑ Where increases in temperature are modest, there will be winners and losers. But there will be only losers if global temperature rises more than 2^0C.

It is believed that there will be impacts on human health (e.g. infectious diseases, heat stress, respiratory diseases) and on food and water security, as well as population displacement (due to droughts and floods) and damage to infrastructure. These impacts could be severe, as they will exacerbate existing problems. For example, water shortages will increase significantly. Food security will be reduced in already critical regions like the Horn of Africa. Some 50 million people worldwide may be displaced in the next five years alone as a result of climatic events (Conisbee and Simms 2003). The very existence of small island states like the Maldives is threatened by flooding and rising sea levels (Munasinghe and Swart 2005).

Catastrophic climatic events also affect employment, even though this is often difficult to quantify. According to the United States Department of Labor, Hurricanes Katrina and Rita resulted in a net of loss of some 40 000 jobs.[58]

---

58   See, for example, Hurricane Katrina and the Employment Situation Report (www.bls.gov/katrina/empsitbrief.htm).

Very little is known about the impact of climate change on industry, and most such information is highly speculative (Munasinghe and Swart 2005). However, it is estimated that the aggregated market sector effects (measured as changes in GDP) will be negative for many developing countries (IPCC 2001). The economic sectors most directly affected would seem to be agriculture, forestry and tourism (Munasinghe and Swart 2005). This is, of course, a serious concern. With well over a billion workers, agriculture continues to be the single largest sector in the world in terms of employment, and most of these jobs are in developing countries (ILO 2003a). Travel and tourism employ some 80 million people directly (3 per cent of total world employment), or about 200 million if suppliers are included. These sectors have been among the fastest growing in terms of employment (ILO 2003b).

Agriculture will probably be faced with more variable crop yields and declining crop yields in the (sub-) tropics. Cereal crop modelling indicates that, in some temperate areas, potential yields will increase with small rises in temperature but will decrease in the case of greater rises. In most tropical and subtropical regions, potential yields are projected to decrease for most projected temperature rises (IPCC 2001). Tourism is affected by extreme events (e.g. cruise ship tourism in the Caribbean drops during the hurricane season) and by permanent changes like beach erosion or lack of snow at ski resorts.

However, there are also likely to be opportunities for job creation, e.g. in reforestation and renewable energies. The development and transfer of environmentally sound technologies could play a critical role in reducing the cost of stabilizing greenhouse gas concentrations, and would therefore need to be supported. In this regard, an increase in energy research and development to help accelerate the development and deployment of advanced environmentally sound energy technologies will be needed (UNEP 2002). Furthermore, the development of renewable energies would not only help to mitigate climate change but also to limit energy price fluctuations and their adverse effects on the labour market.[59]

According to an OECD report, the impacts of current climate change policies on overall employment are likely to be insignificant. A study of the impact of compliance with the very modest emissions reductions in EU countries under the Kyoto Protocol concluded that there will be very little impact on total employment. The main labour market effect will be "churning", as some energy intensive sectors shrink or convert and others grow (OECD 2004), confirming the importance of just transition measures.

Responding to the impacts of climate change: adaptation or mitigation?

Given that climate change is occurring and will continue for a long time, adaptation (i.e. actions intended to reduce its negative effects) will be necessary even if emissions are drastically reduced. Since poor countries and the poor people in these countries are not only the most vulnerable, but also the least able to adapt, adaptation needs to be very location- and sector-specific.

Mitigation refers to actions that reduce the likelihood of climate change or delay its occurrence. The focus of these actions is emissions reductions, primarily of CO_2 and (to a

---

59   See the Introduction by Fatou Ndoye. The issue of new opportunities for environmentally related job creation is addressed in several chapters. This was one of the main issues discussed at the Trade Union Assembly on Labour and the Environment / WILL 2006 in Nairobi.

lesser extent) of methane. These reductions could be achieved through a combination of the following:

- ❑ Greater energy efficiency, while maintaining consumption and production patterns;
- ❑ Use of CO_2 neutral energy sources;
- ❑ Changes in production and consumption patterns;
- ❑ Limiting economic growth.

Which adaptation or mitigation options turn out to have the strongest social and other impacts will depend on the political and economic choices made in the next few years. To a great extent, these choices will also determine trade union agendas.

Some experts maintain that, on present trends, little attention will be paid to mitigation in the foreseeable future. Instead, priority will be given to short-term growth rather than long-term climate concerns. Growth in this case would probably continue to rely largely on conventional fossil fuels, as they would remain the cheapest energy source from the consumers' perspective as well as because of the current supply structure and the high political priority given to ensuring the security of supplies (Egging and van Oostvoorn 2004).

Emerging countries like China and India are projected to increase their energy consumption by 54 per cent by 2020. Thus their CO_2 emissions are likely to increase to meet the needs of economic growth (Nilsson and Bailey 2000). Structural changes already underway would continue, particularly the transfer of more energy intensive primary and manufacturing industries to selected developing countries. Emissions would therefore continue to rise, but their sources would change (Table 3.1.1). Emerging economies as a group are set to become major contributors by 2020, and to overtake industrialized countries as the main emissions source. These countries are not subject to even the limited reduction targets of Annex I Parties under the Kyoto Protocol.[60] With the prospect of high growth and continued reliance on fossil fuels, many hopes for reduced climate impacts are vested in delinking,[61] i.e. reducing the amount of energy needed to generate economic output. Comparisons of energy use on a per capita basis (or per unit GDP) between, for example, the EU, Japan and Brazil on one hand and the United States and China on the other suggest that there is considerable scope for efficiency gains.

Sceptics have pointed out that there are can be diminishing returns on energy savings. After significant progress in reducing resource use was made by industrialized countries in the 1970s and 1980s, this trend was arrested or even reversed (Opschoor 2001). Studies suggest that measures to improve efficiency and curb emissions in developing countries may have been taken earlier than was thought previously. The scope for improvement in developing countries may therefore need to be reconsidered. During periods of very high economic growth, in any case, technological improvements cannot compensate for the volume effect and the overall increase in emissions (Stern 2004).

---

60   The 1997 Kyoto Protocol to the UN Framework Convention on Climate Change commits Annex I Parties to individual, legally binding targets that limit or reduce their emissions of greenhouse gases. Only Parties to the Convention that have also become Parties to the Protocol (i.e by ratifying, accepting, approving, or acceding to it) are bound by the Protocol's commitments. Australia and the United States are the two major countries which signed but did not later ratify the Protocol. 165 countries have ratified the Protocol to date; of these, 35 countries and the European Union are required to reduce GHG emissions below levels specified for each of them in the treaty. Individual targets for Annex I Parties are listed in the Kyoto Protocol's Annex B. They add up to a total cut in GHG emissions of at least 5 per cent from 1990 levels in the commitment period 2008-12 (http://unfccc.int/kyoto_protocol/items/2830.php).http://ec.europa.eu/environment/climat/home_en.htm).

61   Also called decoupling.

Table 3.1.1

World energy consumption and CO2 emissions, 1990-2025

Region	Energy consumption (quadrillion Btu)				CO2 emissions (million metric tonnes)			
	1990	2001	2010	2025	1990	2001	2010	2025
Industrialized countries	182.8	211.5	236.3	281.4	10 462	11 634	12 938	15 643
Eastern Europe/former Soviet Union	76.3	53.3	59.0	75.6	4 902	3 148	3 397	4 313
Developing countries								
Asia	52.5	85.0	110.6	173.4	3 994	6 012	7 647	11 801
Middle East	13.1	20.8	25.0	34.1	846	1 299	1 566	2 110
Africa	9.3	12.4	14.6	21.5	656	843	971	1 413
Central and South America	14.4	20.9	25.4	36.9	703	964	1 194	1 845
Total Developing Countries	89.3	139.2	175.5	265.9	6 200	9 118	11 379	17 168
Total world	348.4	403.9	470.8	622.9	21 563	23 899	27 715	37 124

Source: EIA 2003, 2004.

Measures to reduce emissions to a level that actually stabilizes climate change would have to be far more ambitious than those agreed in the Kyoto Protocol. They would need to address all major emission sources. There are no studies concerning the employment impacts of climate change mitigation on such a scale, either in industrialized countries or in emerging economies and developing countries, which will become the main emissions producers in coming years. Developing countries will face the greatest employment challenge due to growth in their population and in their labour force.

From a social and environmental perspective, a "more of the same" scenario would have three very negative consequences:

❑ A development pattern that generates too little to absorb the growing labour force and that distributes wealth too unevenly to reduce poverty effectively would be perpetuated;
❑ Opportunities to create employment that is sustainable in the long run, and that does not have a high environmental cost, would not be seized;
❑ Climate change would continue and even accelerate, putting off much bigger adjustments until later and increasing the risk of sudden and disruptive change.

Rescuing mitigation: the role of trade unions

The odds seem strongly against mitigation. It is often argued that this is due to "facts" like energy prices, availability, the need for security, and the high cost of (and limited potential for) alternative energy sources. According to proponents of this point of view, prioritizing climate protection and shifting to environmentally friendly energy sources would entail high costs and lead to reductions in growth, development and jobs. This line of argument is dominant, but it is not as compelling as its proponents portray it.

The estimated cost of adopting a set of policy measures that would stabilize emissions at levels that prevent drastic and possibly irreversible climate change is relatively low. For most countries, the "costs associated with mitigation will be limited to a few tenths of a percentage point of projected annual growth rates, dependent on the way policies and measures are combined and implemented" (Munasinghe and Swart 2005). In a similar vein, Scheer (2004) presents evidence from feasibility studies in a number of countries suggesting that transition to renewable energy is both technically and economically feasible.

The real issue may not be so much the feasibility and cost of mitigation, and of transition, but who will pay for it, who will benefit from change and who will not. More work is needed on this question, with respect to both industrialized countries and developing ones, where a case can be made that the potential consequences of trade-offs between economic, environmental and social objectives are even more important.

Trade unions have been emphasizing the need for transition policies to help workers and others adapt to technological and structural changes. The later mitigation starts, the more difficult this will be since the changes will be more disruptive, including for employment. A warning example illustrating this point is the ban on logging in China and other Asian countries in the 1990s. After decades of poor and destructive forest practices, political pressure to act increased after severe floods killed thousands of people. The Chinese Government reacted by banning all logging over vast areas. In that country, over 1 million forest workers lost their jobs and needed assistance to find a new livelihood (ILO 2001).

Early and more continuous adjustment is desirable. The best hope lies in the fact that technology is evolving rapidly, and that many measures become attractive and feasible once all the costs and benefits are considered and advantage is taken of synergies with other policy areas (e.g. energy security and poverty reduction) (Kok and de Coninck 2004, Munasinghe and Swart 2005).

Box 3.1.1

United States: New energy for America – the Apollo Alliance coalition[62]

The Apollo Alliance is a United States-based coalition of labour unions, environmentalists, community advocates and others committed to improving access to good jobs and clean energy. It comprises a widening range of partners with a shared vision of reducing the country's dependence on imported energy, particularly oil, as well as promoting a cleaner environment and encouraging job creation.

The mission of the Apollo Alliance is to build a broad-based constituency in support of a sustainable clean-energy economy that will create millions of good jobs, reduce dependence on foreign oil, and result in cleaner and healthier communities. Through the presentation of policy alternatives, organization, and on-the-ground activities in states and cities across the United States, the Alliance is demonstrating that a socially just, environmentally balanced and economically prosperous future is attainable.

The Alliance was launched in 2003 to unify constituencies behind a bold plan of investment in clean energy technology and sustainable infrastructure that could create jobs, reduce the county's impact on the global environment, and dramatically reduce oil dependence within a generation.

The organization's ten-point plan for energy independence attracted considerable attention, including at the highest political levels in the United States. It entails:

- Promoting advanced technology and hybrid cars;

- Investing in more efficient factories;

- Encouraging high-performance building;

- Increasing the use of energy-efficient appliances;

- Modernization of electrical infrastructure;

- Expansion of renewable energy development;

- Improving transportation options;

- Reinvesting in smart urban growth;

- Planning for a hydrogen future;

- Preserving regulatory protection.

The Apollo Alliance has been active at both state and local levels with a range of initiatives. It has encouraged individual states to work towards making a certain percentage of their energy production renewable.

One of the organization's most important goals is to integrate labour and environmental issues.

---

62 Based on the case study presented by Jerome Ringo, President of the Apollo Alliance, at the Trade Union Assembly on Labour and the Environment / WILL 2006 in Nairobi.

Box 3.1.2

Belgium: Trade union participation in the development of CDM/JI projects [63]

As part of its commitment to a cleaner environment, the Belgian Government has used the Kyoto Protocol's Joint Implementation[64] and Clean Development[65] Mechanisms (JI/CDM) to meet national greenhouse gas emissions reduction targets. The objectives of this initiative have been to create a tool for achieving GHG emissions reductions while supporting social and employment policies.

In formulating a tendering process for these projects, the Government sought input from trade unions, employer associations and NGOs. Steps were taken to monitor projects' environmental, social and economic impacts. The initiative involved the General Federation of Belgian Workers (FGTB), environmental NGOs, local trade unions in countries that were Parties to the project, and project developers. The FGTB took part in planning the tendering process and in monitoring projects. A similar procedure could be used to empower local trade unions in developing countries.

Proposed projects were in Congo, Cyprus, El Salvador, Germany, Hungary, India, Kenya, New Zealand, Russia and Vietnam. The call for Expressions of Interest closed on 23 September 2005: 36 were received, of which 18 successfully passed the first phase of screening. There were 6 JI and 12 CDM projects.

Belgium's Council of Ministers has sought advice in order to achieve a balance between economic, environmental and social impacts. To be accepted, projects have been required to respect the principles of the OECD Guidelines for Multinational Enterprises, the principles and rights set out in the 1998 ILO Declaration on Fundamental Principles and Rights at Work, and ILO Conventions No. 155 on Occupational Health and Safety (1981) and No. 169 on Indigenous and Tribal Peoples (1989).

In terms of these JI/CDM projects, Belgium is becoming one of the world's most proactive countries with respect to social criteria and sustainability.

Plans are monitored with the explicit participation of trade unions. Contracts may be terminated in the event of non-respect of commitments taken relative to the ILO conventions.

---

63 Based on the case study presented by Fred Maes, representing the General Federation of Belgian Workers (FGTB), at the Trade Union Assembly on Labour and the Environment / WILL 2006 in Nairobi.

64 The basic principles of the Joint Implementation Mechanism are defined in Article 6 of the Kyoto Protocol: "For the purpose of meeting its commitments … any Party included in Annex I may transfer to, or acquire from, any other such Party [i.e. Annex I country] emission reduction units resulting from projects aimed at reducing anthropogenic emissions by sources or enhancing anthropogenic removals by sinks of greenhouse gases in any sector of the economy" provided that certain requirements are fulfilled (http://unfccc.int/kyoto_protocol/mechanisms/joint_implementation/items/1674.php).

65 The Clean Development Mechanism (CDM) is defined in Article 12 of the Kyoto Protocol. It provides for Annex I Parties to implement project activities that reduce emissions in non-Annex I Parties in return for certified emission reductions (CERs). The CERs generated by such project activities can be used by Annex I Parties to help meet their emissions targets under the Protocol. Article 12 also stresses that such project activities are to assist the developing country host Parties in achieving sustainable development and in contributing to the ultimate objective of the UN Framework Convention on Climate Change (http://unfccc.int/kyoto_protocol/mechanisms/clean_development_mechanism/items/2718.php).

The need for an integrated perspective: the example of Brazil

Narrow evaluations of the options for growth, energy supply and climate change mitigation run the risk of trade-offs between economic, environmental and social objectives. These trade-offs may not be so much associated with a particular technology as with the way that technology is implemented.

Two renewable energy sources produced on a very large scale in Brazil illustrate this point. Ethanol and charcoal are used for transport and for iron ore processing, respectively. Both have received renewed attention and a strong boost from recent price hikes in fossil fuels and concerns about CO2 emissions.

The two fuels rely on biomass (sugar cane and trees), new crops of which will absorb the emissions released by burning them. They are therefore largely CO2 neutral and their expanded use is a contribution to climate change mitigation. However, what is good for one aspect of the environment, i.e. the climate, is not automatically good for other aspects, such as biodiversity, or social concerns such as employment, income and poverty reduction (Box 3.1.3).

Box 3.1.3

Brazil: Decent work vs. damage to the environment – advantages and disadvantages of large-scale ethanol and carbon production

Ethanol

Brazil is the only country in the world where biofuels are cost-effective and are used on a large scale in the transport sector. Almost all of the United States' oil imports (13.15 million barrels per day in 2004) are used for transport. Biofuels could therefore be an interesting option for the US, as well as for smaller oil importing countries, e.g. in Africa and Latin America (Kok and de Coninck 2004).

The Brazilian ethanol programme was launched in the wake of the oil price shock of 1974. While it is often presented as a success story and a potential model for other countries, this may be an oversimplification of a complex process in which a number of mistakes were made and there was a mixed outcome. The programme was economically viable in the period 1976-81. Then oil prices fell and the ethanol industry depended on subsidies to keep it alive until 2003, when oil prices rose again. The role of the state has been decisive in developing the ethanol industry and keeping it alive.

The ethanol programme created many jobs in its early phases, which was an important factor in its positive overall evaluation. The quality of these jobs was often questionable. Problems included child and bonded labour, seasonality and poor work safety. Important social dimensions that have received less attention include income and asset distribution. Problematic environmental dimensions have included large-scale monocultures, use of hazardous chemicals, and the large amounts of water needed in processing.

Brazil is the world's largest sugar producer. Half of its production is used for ethanol. There are some 50 000 producers in Brazil, but much of the sugar cane used for ethanol today is grown on big estates, between them covering hundreds of square kilometres with a single crop. In the mid 1990s, the 400 owners of ethanol distilleries produced 62 per cent of all their raw material (Macedo 2006). Sugar production has been mechanized, probably improving job quality. However, employment generation effects appear to be much smaller today. While about 800 000 jobs were directly linked to ethanol production in 1991, employment has fallen by about one-quarter. Most jobs have been lost in crop production, particularly cane harvesting. This drop is associated with reduced seasonality, relatively good wages and a high proportion of formal employment, at least in the south-east of the country (Macedo 2006).

Despite reductions in job numbers, ethanol is a very employment intensive energy source compared to others. The relative numbers of jobs/unit energy are petroleum=1, coal=4, hydroelectricity=3 and ethanol=150. If production takes place on a smaller scale, this figure is even higher. Ethanol also has the highest rate of energy output/input of any biomass fuel.

An oil import-substituting biofuel programme could be interesting for many countries. Manufacturing has often been rendered unviable by globalization, leading to deindustrialization. Agriculture and agro-processing are among the few areas with potential for development. However, products are often not competitive on crowded international markets. Import substitution of oil could avoid that competition. If it is viable to rely on networks of family farms rather than industrial estates, this could also contribute to poverty alleviation and avoid large-scale monocultures. Such outcomes are not merely determined by technology and prices, but are also subject to prevailing interests and power relations.

Charcoal

Charcoal is much less well-known than ethanol as a renewable energy source for industry, but it is used on a very large scale in Brazil, which is one of the world's largest iron producers. Charcoal has traditionally been used in the state of Minas Gerais to process iron ore. In the last few decades it has also been used for this purpose in the state of Pará in Amazonia. Charcoal recently received a major boost due to rising energy prices and climate concerns.

Charcoal production near the large iron ore deposits in Carajás in Amazonia has led to the conversion of vast areas of natural forests. Today almost two-thirds of the charcoal comes from plantations of fast-growing trees (e.g. eucalyptus). Most plantations are large, concentrating access to productive resources and sharply reducing biodiversity. There are reportedly some 140 000 jobs associated with growing and harvesting wood for charcoal, and another 65 000 in charcoal making (ABRACAVE 2001). Although wages are low, operations are increasingly mechanized, reducing their employment generation effect. There have been persistent problems with child labour and bonded labour in charcoal making (Brazil, Ministério público do trabalho 2001).

In 2005, charcoal production jumped 20 per cent. This was partly the result of price increases for substitutes, but the main driver was the opportunity to produce "green iron" that does not contribute to climate change, and to sell credits for avoided emissions to other industries and countries. Some projects are being implemented under the Clean Development Mechanism (CDM), but their social impact leaves much to be desired. As in the case of ethanol, this activity is very positive from a climate change perspective. Nevertheless, it should be assessed from a broader sustainable development point of view to ensure that solving one problem does not create others. To profit from this opportunity may require changing the criteria and the incentive structure of the CDM, which currently consider only carbon emissions reductions.

A study of more than 100 development projects, concerning ways to strengthen adaptive capacity to climate change, arrives at very similar conclusions (Mortimore and Manvell 2006). The poor are those most affected. Integrated approaches are needed to enhance adaptive capacity, including diversification beyond agriculture to other sources of employment and income. Solutions cannot simply be found in technical "fixes". The participation of those involved in decision-making and institutions, their access to resources and the distribution of benefits are all key variables for positive outcomes.

The way ahead

Energy and climate change are two central policy areas for sustainable development. They have major implications for employment, income distribution and poverty. There are strong indications that coherent policies, taking into account trade-offs and synergies between policy objectives, would reduce climate change, lower the cost of mitigation and improve social outcomes.

Unfortunately, climate and energy policies are too often discussed in isolation, with little regard for the social implications of the policies or development patterns adopted. This neglect of the social dimension is one reason for the major knowledge gaps that exist concerning the social impacts of climate change itself, and those of adaptation or mitigation. Knowledge of the social impacts associated with mitigation is particularly important with respect to emerging economies and developing countries, where emissions will increase rapidly at the same time that large and growing populations are looking for better livelihoods.

Trade unions have played an important role in pointing out the need for an integrated analysis and coherent policies. It is vital for them to continue to raise this issue and to build alliances with other groups for integrated approaches, for rapid implementation of no-regrets policies, and for energy policies that lead to sustainable employment and income (Box 3.1.4).

Institutions, equity considerations and active participation are all essential for strategies' adoption and successful implementation. Trade unions have demonstrated the potential of their contribution at the workplace, community and national level. Many approaches, instruments and institutional channels are known and documented (e.g. see UNCSD 2006). The contributions of trade unions will be even more important in the future.

Box 3.1.4

Germany: The Alliance for Work and the Environment[66]

The way technologies are embedded in a national and local context is a major factor in determining their contribution to sustainable development. Trade unions can play a major role in this regard – at national, local and enterprise levels. There are numerous examples of "no regrets" approaches which contribute to climate change mitigation, as well as to employment. A number of these approaches can be found in the trade union submission to the UN Commission on Sustainable Development in 2006).[67]

A positive example of this approach is the Alliance for Work and the Environment in Germany. A joint initiative by trade unions, employers, government and environmental groups, it aims to improve insulation in 300 000 apartments. This will create 200 000 jobs, save 2 million tonnes of CO_2 emissions and reduce heating bills. Total benefits from reduced unemployment, reduced heating and increased taxes are estimated at US$4 billion, produced through initial government funding of only US$1.8 billion.

---

66 Based on the case study presented by Werner Schneider, representing the Deutscher Gewerkschaftsbund (DBG), at the Trade Union Assembly on Labour and the Environment / WILL 2006 in Nairobi.
67 http://webapps01.un.org/dsd/caseStudy/public/Welcome.do.

References

- ABRACAVE (2001). Mão-de-obra empregada na siderurgia a carvão vegetal no Brasil (Sociedade Brasiliera de Silicultura) (www.sbs.org.br/estatisticas.htm).

- Apollo Alliance (2004). New Energy for America: Apollo Jobs Report (www.apolloalliance.org/docUploads/ApolloReport%5F022404%5F122748%2Epdf).

- Brazil, Ministerio público do trabalho (2001). Trabalho escravo/forçado, trabalho indígena, Relatório de atividades 2001.

- Conisbee, Molly and Andrew Simms (2003). Environmental Refugees: The Case for Recognition. New Economics Foundation (nef), London (www.neweconomics.org/gen/uploads/lpce0g55xjx5eq55mfjxbb5523102003180040.pdf).

- Egging, Rudolf G. and Frits van Oostvoorn (2004). The energy supply: security and climate change. In Kok and de Coninck 2004.

- EIA (Energy Information Agency) (2005). International Energy Outlook (official energy statistics from the United States Government) (www.eia.doe.gov/environment.html).

- Hall, Charles, Dietmar Ledergerber, Reiner Kümmel, Timm Kroeger and Wolfgang Eichhorn (2001). The Need to Reintegrate the Natural Sciences with Economics. BioScience 51:8 (August) (www.ker.co.nz/pdf/Need_to_reintegrate.pdf).

- Houghton, John T. and others (2001). Climate Change 2001: The Scientific Basis (This is the first volume of the IPCC Assessment. See IPCC 2001, below).

- ILO (International Labour Organization) (2001). Globalization and sustainability – the forestry and wood industries on the move. Report for Discussion at the Tripartite Meeting on the Social and Labour Dimensions of the Forestry and Wood Industries on the Move, Geneva, 2001 (www.ilo.org/public/english/dialogue/sector/techmeet/tmfwi01/tmfwir.pdf).

— (2003a). Decent Work in Agriculture. Background Report for the International Workers' Symposium on Decent Work in Agriculture, Geneva, 15-18 September 2003 (www.ilo.org/public/english/dialogue/actrav/new/agsymp03/iwsdwa.pdf).

— (2003b). New threats to employment in the travel and tourism industry – 2003 (www.ilo.org/public/english/dialogue/sector/papers/tourism/emp2003.pdf).

— (2006). Global Employment Trends Brief, January 2006 (www.ilo.org/public/english/employment/strat/download/getb06en.pdf).

- IPCC (Intergovernmental Panel on Climate Change) (2001). Third Assessment Report – Climate Change 2001 (The Scientific Basis; Impacts, Adaptation and Vulnerability; Mitigation; Synthesis Report) (www.grida.no/climate/ipcc_tar). These reports may be downloaded from the IPPC website in Arabic, Chinese, English, French, Russian and Spanish. Unofficial translations into Danish, Japanese and German may also be downloaded from this site.

- Kok, M.T.J. and H.C. de Coninck (eds.) (2004). Beyond Climate – Options for Broadening Climate Policy. Netherlands Research Programme on Climate Change, Report 500036 001. National Institute for Public Health and the Environment, Bilthoven (www.rivm.nl/bibliotheek/rapporten/500036001.pdf).

- Lee Chien-Chiang (2006). The causality relationship between energy consumption and GDP in G-11 countries revisited. Energy Policy 34.

- Macedo, Isaias C. (undated). Energía da cana de açucar no Brasil. Universidade Estadual de Campinas, São Paulo, Brazil (www.rau-tu.unicamp/nou-rau/sbu/document/list.php?tid=12). (Also see: www.unica.com.br.pages.sociedade mercado3.asp, and, in English: www.undp.org/energy/publications/1995/1995a_ch10.htm.)

References (...cont'd)

— Macedo, Isaias C.(2005) Etanol combustível: balanço e perspectives. UNICAMP, Campinas (www.nipeuunicamp.org.br/proalcool/Palestras/).

• May, Peter, Emily Boyd, Fernanco Veiga and Manyu Chang (2004). Local Sustainable Development Effects of Forest Carbon Projects in Brazil and Bolivia: A View from the Field. Environmental Economics Programme, International Institute for Environment and Development (IIED) (www.rlc.fao.org/foro/psa/pdf/susta.pdf). Copies of this paper may also be ordered from Earthprint, Stevenage, UK.

• Mortimore, Michael and Adam Manvell (2006). Climate Change: Enhancing Adaptive Capacity. Natural Resource Systems Programme (NRSP), Department for International Development (DFID), Hemel Hempstead, UK (www.napa-pana.org/extranapa/UserFiles/File/FTR%20Annex%20K%20Brief_LR.pdf).

• Munasinghe, Mohan and Rob Swart (2005). Primer on Climate Change and Sustainable Development: Facts, Policy Analysis, and Applications. Cambridge University Press, Edinburgh.

• Musser, George (2005). The Climax of Humanity. Editorial in Scientific American. September.

• Nilsson L.J. and O. Bailey (2000). Energy Services and Development. In Luis Gómez-Echeverri (ed.), Climate Change and Development. Yale School of Forestry and Environmental Studies, New Haven, USA.

• OECD (Organisation for Economic Cooperation and Development) (2004). Environment and Employment: An Assessment. Environment Policy Committee (EPOC) Working Party on National Environmental Policy. ENV/EPOC/WPNEP (2003)/11.FINAL (www.oecd.org/dataoecd/13/44/31951962.pdf).

• Opschoor, Hans (2001). Economic growth, the environment and welfare: are they compatible? In R. Seroa de Motta (ed.), Environmental Economics and Policy Making in Developing Countries: Current Issues. Elgar, Cheltenham, UK.

• Pearce, Fred (2006). Atmospheric CO2 accumulating faster than ever. New Scientist (15 March).

• Scheer, Hermann (2004). Energy Autonomy: New Politics for Renewable Energy. Earthscan, London.

• Stern, David I. (2004). The Rise and Fall of the Environmental Kuznets Curve. World Development 32:8, pp.1419-39 (www.rpi.edu/~sternd/WD2004.pdf).

• UNCSD (United Nations Commission on Sustainable Development) (2006). Contribution by Workers and Trade Unions. United Nations Economic and Social Council, Commission for Sustainable Development, 14th Session, 1-12 May 2006 (Doc. E/CN.17/2006/5/Add.6) (http://daccessdds.un.org/doc/UNDOC/GEN/N05/620/63/PDF/N0562063.pdf?OpenElement).

• UNEP (United Nations Environment Programme) (2002). Global Environment Outlook (GEO-3) (www.unep.org/geo/geo3).

• Wilson, E.O. (2002). E.O. Wilson and the future of life, interview with Ben Wattenberg on "Think Tank". Public Broadcasting System (PBS), United States, 12 December (www.pbs.org/thinktank/transcript1021.html).

• WMO (World Meteorological Organization) (2006). WMO Greenhouse Gas Bulletin: The State of Greenhouse Gases in the Atmosphere Using Global Observations up to December 2004, No. 1 (14 March) (www.wmo.ch/web/arep/gaw/ghg/ghg-bulletin-en-03-06.pdf).

• World Bank (2005). World Development Indicators 2005.

3.2. Access to public utilities

Shizue Tomoda, Sectoral Activities (SECTOR), International Labour Organization

The vital role of public utilities

Regulatory and structural changes have taken place with respect to public utilities in the last few decades, particularly regarding electricity and gas provision (ILO 1999a, b, 2001, 2003). Formerly public or private monopolies, they have gradually been opened up as a result of liberalization. Water, electricity and gas utilities have a vital role to play not only in the provision of basic services, but also in the growth of other economic sectors and the development of society as a whole. It is in the public interest that basic services are supplied to all citizens, regardless of type of ownership. However, access to these services, particularly clean water, is often still inadequate. Inequalities persist between and within countries. Ensuring universal access to clean water, which is vital to human health and survival, remains a challenge, especially in developing countries.

In many countries where freshwater has long been considered a free commodity, it may be difficult to accept the idea that water for drinking and other purposes is an economic good, with distribution costs which must be paid if this service is to remain economically sustainable. Globally, the amount of available freshwater per person fell from 16 800 m3/person/year in 1950 to 6800 m3/person/year in 2000. As population and per capita demand for freshwater increase, the share of the world population living in countries with water stress will grow which means there will be further negative impacts on food production, the transmission of diseases and economic development in these countries.[68]

Over a billion people do not have access to improved water supplies.[69] At least 2.5 billion (out of a world population of almost 6.7 billion) do not have access to adequate sanitation.[70] Throughout history, in many parts of the world, access to water has been a potential source of conflict; while this is still the case, the need for water can also be a catalyst for regional cooperation and development (ILO 1999b). A key question remains: How will people be provided with the minimum services they require for basic health and survival in the future?

During the last few decades, economic pressure and increasing global competition have affected public services throughout the world. Public services in developing countries have been seriously impacted, particularly under pressure from structural adjustment programmes imposed (against a backdrop of growing national deficits) by international lending institutions. Restructuring of public utilities has usually preceded privatization in efforts to improve these services.

---

68 World Health Organization figures (www.euro.who.int/globalchange).

69 Improved drinking water sources include household connections, public standpipes, boreholes, protected dug wells, protected springs, and rainwater collections. Unimproved water sources are unprotected wells, unprotected springs, vendor-provided water, bottled water (unless water for other uses is available from an improved source) and tanker truck-provided water (www.who.int/whosis/whostat2006ImprovedWaterImprovedSanitation.pdf).

70 "About one-third of the world's population lives in countries suffering from moderate-to-high water stress – where water consumption is more than 10 per cent of renewable freshwater resources. Some 80 countries, constituting 40 per cent of the world's population, were suffering from serious water shortages by the mid-1990s. Increasing water demand has been caused by population growth, industrial development and the expansion of irrigated agriculture. For many of the world's poorer populations, one of the greatest environmental threats to health remains the continued use of untreated water. While the percentage of people served with improved water supplies increased from 79 per cent (4.1 billion) in 1990 to 82 per cent (4.9 billion) in 2000, 1.1 billion people still lack access to safe drinking water and 2.4 billion lack access to adequate sanitation. Most of these people are in Africa and Asia. Lack of access to safe water supply and sanitation results in hundreds of millions of cases of water-related diseases, and more than 5 million deaths, every year." Excerpted from UNEP 2002 ("GEO-3"), p. xxii).

Whatever option is chosen for service improvement, the conclusions adopted in 2001 at the ILO Joint Meeting on the Impact of Decentralization and Privatization on Municipal Services underscore the importance of transparency in regard to information and procedures, and of participation in such processes by workers' representatives to ensure that there are positive results for all stakeholders (Box 3.2.1).

Box 3.2.1

The impact of decentralizing and privatizing public utilities

Decentralization and privatization of public services can seriously affect the terms of employment and working conditions of public service workers. In the context of public service reforms, decentralization and privatization are often regarded as important means to achieve improved efficiency and quality service delivery. However, decentralized public services do not necessarily function smoothly in many areas. For example, there may be imbalances in financial resources within a country. Consequently, municipalities and local governments may opt for a variety of approaches to the privatization of services.

The 2001 ILO Joint Meeting on the Impact of Decentralization and Privatization on Municipal Services addressed such issues in regard to education, health, transport and utility services.

Participants concluded that public service reforms at all levels – and in all forms – should be such that:

- Access to safe, reliable and affordable public services is ensured;

- Sustainable local economic and social development is facilitated, with the aim of full employment and poverty alleviation;

- Universal and equitable access to all necessary public services is provided in order to fulfil basic human needs;

- A healthy environment is safeguarded;

- There is improvement and enhancement of democracy and the security of human rights.

They also agreed that public service reforms must be guided by the following basic principles:

- Accountability, transparency and openness of government policies and actions, to ensure the integrity of government programmes and procurement;

- Provision of new or better public services;

- The importance of maintaining and creating good working conditions and the application of core labour standards during the reform process, to ensure sustained morale among workers and the delivery of quality public services;

- Social dialogue with all relevant stakeholders, as a prerequisite for designing, implementing and evaluating decentralization and privatization;

- Provision of adequate resources and training to enhance informed decision-making;

- Valuing the diversity of different communities and cultures;

- Ensuring equal opportunity for all.

ILO Joint Meeting on the Impact of Decentralization and Privatization on Municipal Services (2001) www.ilo.org/public/english/dialogue/sector/techmeet/jmms01/jmmsn.pdf

The importance of strengthening public accountability during and after restructuring and privatization processes, in order to prevent deterioration of the quality of and access to utility services, was also emphasized at this meeting (ILO 2001).

Privatization and public-private partnerships

Privatization of utilities has been encouraged during the last few decades because of the widespread belief that, where public debts have accumulated, the private sector can deliver services much more efficiently than the public sector (i.e. through new investment). A number of multinational companies have therefore won contracts. These companies have gone into developing countries as investors with a firm conviction that their investments would be beneficial to the development of the host countries, as well as to their own global expansion. However, when privatized enterprises have had to comply with the principle of universal access – and to accept the decisions of regulatory institutions (e.g. on rate fixing) – many have realized the difficulty of making investments adequate for the kind of service improvement intended, particularly in countries where per capita income has still been quite low (to the extent that significant tariff hikes to ensure quick returns on investment would be impossible).

In countries where regulatory bodies have not functioned properly, tariffs have often been increased to levels beyond what ordinary customers could bear. Those unable to pay have been denied access, resulting in deteriorated service delivery as well as unsatisfactory returns to investors. The utility services have become economically unsustainable; by the time investors have decided to withdraw altogether from host countries, people in affected areas have often been left with unreliable services of poor quality or with services they could not afford. Throughout the world there are many such examples of the failure of privatized public utilities, mainly due to dysfunctional or incompetent regulatory institutions (Palast and others 2000).

Several conditions must be met if regulatory institutions are to function adequately, and if economically sustainable quality service delivery is to be ensured while meeting the principle of universal access (Palast and others 2000). Institutions need to be operated according to open and democratic processes, with pertinent information made public. Such information may include amounts invested, profits, amounts of pollution emitted (by pollutant), labour costs and salaries.

Some principles must also be adhered to, particularly in the process of fixing new tariffs. These principles include:

- ❑ Observance of "due process" rights of participation and transparency, where anyone with an interest in utility rates (e.g. those interested in environmental protection, protection of the poor, economic development, or employment and labour issues) may participate in the process;
- ❑ Just and reasonable rates (e.g. making it possible for poor families to afford utility services more easily, or to hold investors' profit to a level deemed reasonable given the low levels of risk they have assumed) and prices related to costs;
- ❑ No arbitrary confiscation of investments without due process of law;
- ❑ Balancing of various interests by regulators, with investors at one end of the see-saw and many competing interests (e.g. social equity, environmental protection, labour, consumer protection) at the other end.

As illustrated by the above principles, private sector enterprises that deliver public services are unable to operate purely with a profit-making management style and strategies. They are compelled to adhere to the principle of universal access and to be governed by the decisions of regulatory institutions. Due to a number of failed cases of privatization in public services (compounded by political and economic uncertainty in countries where investment opportunities might exist), investors have become more cautious about overseas investments in public services.

Against that backdrop, other alternative measures such as public-private partnerships (PPPs) have recently been promoted and implemented to improve the efficiency of public service delivery. One principle of this type of partnership is that public and private interests allocate risks and enjoy benefits proportionately, while assisting the partners to operate and develop in their specialty areas. For example, the private sector's management skills and financial expertise could help to operate public services more efficiently. The problem is that there are often imbalances in capacity between partners, to the extent that the partnership may not function ideally (Beaulieu 2003).

For any PPP to work well, the partnership should be developed based on democratic regulation, with public and private interests able to bargain on equal terms. Resource support for long-haul participation, and familiarity with procedural and technical aspects and regulation through adequate training, are necessary if negotiations are to take place on an equal footing. Participatory and transparent bargaining must reflect the public interest and result in enforceable rules for the partnership (Oppenheim and MacGregor 2004).

The general assumption that the private sector performs more efficiently than the public sector has been crucial in justifying the promotion of PPPs. However, studies on public and private sector efficiency in water services (covering both developing and developed countries) released by international and regional lending institutions such as the International Monetary Fund, the World Bank and the Asian Development Bank show that no consistent conclusion can be drawn based on the evidence gathered, and that there is "no systematic significant difference between public and private operators in terms of efficiency or other performance measures" (Hall and Lobina 2005). One conclusion of these studies is that a change from public to private ownership is not necessarily a solution for an underperforming service.

Proper assessment of benefits, effects and costs before undertaking privatization could help to avoid problems arising from short-term political considerations. Public benefit assessment could include financial and budgetary considerations, as well as implications for economic and regional development. Environmental impacts, social welfare, equity issues, implications for consumers, and the full range of employment and labour issues (covering such topics as employment levels, working conditions, industrial relations, occupational safety and public health) should also be considered (Box 3.2.2).

Consequently, privatization cannot be a substitute for the state's responsibility to ensure basic services to all, whether these services are provided publicly or privately.

Positive and negative impacts of restructuring the energy supply

In the context of growing demand, the various forms of restructuring underway in many countries (including privatization) can have both positive and negative environmental effects. Economic pressure may prevent companies from investing in renewable and energy-efficient programmes. Companies seeking short-term profitability may resort to technologies that actually generate more pollution (ILO 1999b). However, use of new technologies (e.g. to generate clean electricity) may curtail environmental damage.

Technologies that can be used to generate renewable energy are considered an effective means of expanding the energy supply base without costly investment or the need for highly skilled experts to operate installations. Not only can these technologies help reinforce the capacity of local industry, but they can also contribute to employment generation. They may make it possible to create small-scale energy production installations that can easily be run by local communities in developed or developing countries.

Decentralization of the energy supply can contribute to the growth of small and medium-scale industries and businesses in rural areas, where inhabitants often depend on a subsistence level income. Such operations, if managed properly, could form a basis for income in rural communities.

Other benefits include revitalization of rural areas, leading to improvement in the quality of inhabitants' lives, health and education, and an associated slowing of migration to urban areas. Related technologies (e.g. for irrigation, crop drying and communications systems to improve marketing) could also be used to improve agriculture.

Governments and public reforms

Governments have a critical role to play in addressing the employment, environmental and social impacts of restructuring and privatization. Their crucial role is recognized not only with respect to the provision of utility services to the public, but also as employers and owners (e.g. when deciding to restructure or privatize these services) and as custodians of the environment. Governments should be accountable for driving the consultative process, and for developing effective regulatory and monitoring mechanisms.

Governments also play a key role in providing a social safety net, particularly for workers affected by restructuring and privatization, including in the context of moving towards cleaner technologies. Although the extent to which governments may be able to provide such a safety net varies in accordance with the economic and political situation in the country concerned, they should (if required by their social partners) develop trust funds and other measures for retraining and for handling redundancies. A registry of displaced workers could be maintained and matched with job opportunities in the labour market. Assistance could also be given to workers starting small economically sustainable businesses.

Agreements on setting aside a percentage of revenues generated by privatization for compensation packages and the retraining of displaced workers are practical means of mitigating the negative employment and social consequences of restructuring, privatization and the transition to sustainable production patterns. Framework agreements and guidelines become very important when all parties concerned jointly address a host of social, employment and environmental issues relating to (and arising from) the restructuring and privatization of public utility enterprises.

Social dialogue as a prerequisite for public service reforms

Social dialogue is an essential prerequisite for designing, implementing and evaluating any reforms of public services. Social dialogue is not a one-off event, but a continuous process of consultation, as well as of negotiation between workers' representatives and employers from the public and private sectors. It does not end with the implementation of a reform, but should continue to ensure that the intended outcome is carried out.

It is critical for public services, whether delivered publicly or privately, to be governed within a regulatory framework consistent with these basic guiding principles. Concluding such a framework between the social partners at the national and local levels, as well as between a municipality and service providers, is imperative in order to ensure that quality, access, safety and environmental standards relating to service delivery are met. Strong regulatory bodies are also required.

As indicated earlier, public utility services are essential. They play a vital role in economic and social development. Publicly or privately provided, they must serve the public interest (ILO 2003). Governments are ultimately responsible for ensuring reliable universal access and the continuity of services, within transparent and accountable regulatory frameworks. Increased competition and globalization in the public utilities sector in recent years have forced changes in regulatory frameworks and in the ownership structures of enterprises, as well as business diversification of such enterprises. These changes have had an impact on job security and working conditions in the utilities sector. Technological innovations can improve work efficiency, but an adequate level of staffing and sufficient training in the use of new technologies are still important to ensure efficiency, health and safety at the workplace. They are also important if enterprises are to remain competitive. Adoption of good governance and corporate social responsibility (CSR) by enterprises is also encouraged, as they could provide strategies and initiatives for applying best practices, particularly when addressing social and employment issues at the time of restructuring.

The tripartite constituents of the public utilities sector share an interest in the sustainable supply of skilled and productive labour to this sector, as the age profile and gender imbalance in many countries are increasing. All parties therefore have the responsibility to make the utilities sector attractive to young and motivated women and men, so that they will enter and remain there, by offering decent working conditions and good career prospects through adequate training to meet changing skill requirements.

Again, whether services are provided publicly or privately, it is essential that they are provided in the public interest, within democratic and transparent regulatory systems. Various employment and labour issues arising from any structural changes in operators must be dealt with through social dialogue between the social partners from the earliest possible stage, in compliance with the ILO's core conventions,[71] in order to try to mitigate any negative impact of reforms and to find optimal solutions for both parties.

Social dialogue remains the means by which all parties concerned should be able to develop mutually beneficial solutions to the socio-economic, employment and environmental challenges posed by the changing global economic environment.

---

71   The ILO "core" conventions are enshrined in the ILO Declaration on Fundamental Principles and Rights at Work, adopted by the ILO in 1998 and commonly referred to as "the Declaration". It is an expression of commitment by governments, as well as employers' and workers' organizations, to uphold basic human values that are vital to our social and economic lives. The Declaration covers four areas: 1) freedom of association and the right to collective bargaining; 2) elimination of forced and compulsory labour; 3) abolition of child labour; 4) elimination of discrimination in the workplace (www.ilo.org/dyn/declaris/DECLARATIONWEB.INDEXPAGE).

References

- Beaulieu, Jean (2003). Challenges and opportunities facing public utilities. Report for discussion at the Tripartite Meeting on Challenges and Opportunities Facing Public Utilities. ILO, Geneva (www.ilo.org/public/english/dialogue/sector/techmeet/tmcopu03/tmcopu-r.pdf).

- Hall, David and Emanuele Lobina (2005). The relative efficiency of public and private sector water. Public Services International Research Unit (PSIRU), Business School, University of Greenwich, London (www.psiru.org/reports/2005-10-W-effic.doc).

- ILO (International Labour Organization) (1999a). Note on the Proceedings, Tripartite Meeting on Managing the Privatization and Restructuring of Public Utilities, Geneva, 12-16 April (www.ilo.org/public/english/dialogue/sector/techmeet/tmpu99/tmpun.htm).

— (1999b). Managing the Privatization and Restructuring of Public Utilities (Water, Gas and Electricity), Report for discussion at the Tripartite Meeting on Managing the Privatization and Restructuring of Public Utilities, Geneva (www.ilo.org/public/english/dialogue/sector/techmeet/tmpure1.htm).

— (2001). Note on the Proceedings, Joint Meeting on the Impact of Decentralization and Privatization on Municipal Services, Geneva, 15-19 October (www.ilo.org/public/english/dialogue/sector/techmeet/jmms01/jmmsn.pdf).

— (2003). Note on the Proceedings, Tripartite Meeting on Challenges and Opportunities Facing Public Utilities, Geneva, 19-23 May (www.ilo.org/public/english/dialogue/sector/techmeet/tmcopu03/tmcopu-n.pdf).

- Oppenheim, Jerrold and Theo MacGregor (2004). Democracy and Public-Private Partnership. Sectoral Working Paper No. 213. ILO, Geneva (www.ilo.org/public/english/dialogue/sector/papers/utilit/wp213.pdf).

- Palast, Gregory, J. Oppenheim and T. MacGregor (2000). Democratic Regulation: A Guide to the Control of Privatized Public Services through Social Dialogue. Sectoral Working Paper No. 166. ILO, Geneva (www.ilo.org/public/english/dialogue/sector/papers/pubserve/demreg.pdf).

- UNEP (United Nations Environment Programme) (2002). Global Environment Outlook (GEO-3) (www.unep.org/geo/geo3).

3.3. Occupational, environmental and public health

Ivan D. Ivanov, Occupational Health Programme (SDE/PHE), World Health Organization, **Igor Fedotov***, International Programme for Safety and Health at Work and the Environment (SafeWork), International Labour Organization, and* **Monika Wehrle-MacDevette***, Division of Regional Cooperation, United Nations Environment Programme*

From public health to workers' health

Health, as defined in the Constitution of the World Health Organization (WHO), is "a state of complete physical, mental and social well-being and not merely the absence of disease or infirmity." Furthermore, "the highest attainable standard of health is a fundamental right of every human being without distinction of race, religion, political belief, economic or social condition" (WHO 1948). Some aspects of health are also considered to be global public goods, together with knowledge, peace, natural resources, international regulations and standards.

The greatest achievements in reducing morbidity and mortality during the last two centuries in industrialized countries have been due to public health interventions, such as vaccinations against major infectious disease and the provision of safe water and sanitation.

Public health is "the science and art of preventing disease, prolonging life and promoting health through the organized efforts and informed choices of society,

© *Ken Williams / UNEP*

Firefighters tackle a blazing oil tanker, UK: *Firefighting is rigorous work under hazardous conditions with long, irregular hours. Motor vehicles in the United States alone consume more than 120 billion gallons of petrol per year, resulting in over a billion tons of CO2 pollution. Oil extraction lays waste to many fragile ecosystems, harming tropical forests, deserts, wetlands, coastal areas, tundra and arctic coastal plains.*

organizations, public and private, communities and individuals."[72] Unlike clinical health care, public health focuses on groups of people (rather than individuals) and on prevention (rather than treatment) of disease. It includes occupational and environmental health, but also other functions such as combating communicable disease or maternal and child health. Every country needs to ensure some essential public health functions in order to protect the health of its population. With regard to workers' health, essential public health functions include:

❏ Occupational health and safety;
❏ Surveillance of workers' health;
❏ Promotion of workplace health;

---

72 Quoted from Independent Inquiry into Inequalities in Health (the "Acheson Report"), United Kingdom, 1998 (www. archive.official-documents.co.uk/document/doh/ih/ih.htm).

- Planning and delivery of workers' health programmes;
- Training and education;
- Development of a culture of life and health;
- Development of policies, legislation and enforcement;
- Ensuring equitable access to workers' health services;
- Development of human resources and research;
- Addressing the impacts of industrial and agricultural activities on the health of workers' families and neighbouring populations.

Why deal with workers' health? There are about 3 billion workers in the world, or about one-half of the global population. It is estimated that nearly 50 per cent of these workers are working in unhealthy and unsafe conditions. About 170 million children between 5 and 17 years of age work in hazardous environments. Poor working conditions result in a significant burden of disease and death (Box 3.3.1). Every year there are 160 million new cases of work-related illness and 1.9 million people die because of workplace risks and accidents. This is more deaths than from malaria or traffic accidents. Occupational risks determine 15 per cent of asthma deaths and 13 per cent of chronic obstructive pulmonary disease, 13 per cent of cardiovascular disease, 10 per cent of cancer and 8 per cent of injuries (WHO 2002).

Box 3.3.1

Occupational health and safety: gender distribution

Men perform a large majority of hazardous jobs and therefore suffer some 80 per cent of occupational deaths. In high-income countries this figure is 86 per cent; in low-income countries, where communicable disease is much more common, the gender distribution is likely to be more balanced. Recent household surveys carried out in several countries point out that, in traditional agriculture, accident and disease rates are more evenly distributed between genders. However, the outcomes that cause long-term disabilities and absences from work, such as musculo-skeletal disorders, are more common in female than male workers, and the corresponding jobs are often associated with low salary levels (ILO 2005).

Furthermore, workers' health interventions are cost-effective. For example, lack of workers' health protection leads to an annual loss of 4 per cent of GDP (e.g. US$66 billion in the EU15 before 2004). Some corporations have found that for every dollar spent on comprehensive health programmes for workers there was a saving of US$4.56. A study commissioned by WHO demonstrated that in all regions the costs of occupational health interventions for lower back pain are worthwhile and good value for money, as they add years of healthy life to average life expectancy.

The environment and human health

The world is experiencing:

- Unprecedented rates of change in the global environment (e.g. climate change and biodiversity loss);
- The development, dissemination and disposal of new products and technologies (e.g. genetic engineering, nanotechnology);
- The development and consumption of new energy sources;
- An increase in the number, uses and disposal of chemicals.

All these trends contribute to new environmental health risks. They may range from the emergence and global spread of new infections, to new (or more widespread) forms of exposure to physical, chemical, radiation or psychosocial hazards. Environmental contributors to workers' health need to be considered in parallel with workplace health issues.

The recent WHO health synthesis of the Millennium Ecosystem Assessment (MA) report summarizes the findings from the MA's global and sub-global assessments of how ecosystem changes do, or could, affect human health and well-being. It underlines how modern-day advances in health and well-being are placed at risk by the degradation of ecosystem "services" – the complex biological mechanisms that sustain clean air and water resources. Some 60 per cent of the world's vital ecosystem services are already degraded or being subjected to unsustainable pressures. Health impacts from such pressures are being felt, particularly in poor and vulnerable populations. At a glance (WHO 2006):

❑ *Unsafe water and sanitation and poor hygiene* are responsible for almost 90 per cent of the burden of diarrhoeal diseases, which kill almost 1.8 million people per year;
❑ *Solid fuel use and exposure to ambient air pollution* are associated with over one-third of the disease burden from lower respiratory infections;
❑ Urban air pollution (exposure to fine particulates emitted by vehicles, industry and energy generation) is responsible for quantifiable increases in daily and long-term premature mortality due to cardiopulmonary diseases, acute respiratory infections and cancers;
❑ *Climate change* is responsible for deaths and injuries from more extreme weather events (e.g. heat waves, floods and droughts), impacts on regional food production, and changed transmission patterns of vector-borne and other infectious diseases;
❑ *Lead exposure* contributes to childhood mental retardation and to cardiovascular diseases associated with high blood pressure, together causing a loss of almost 13 million disability-adjusted life-years (DALYs) annually, or nearly 1 per cent of the global burden of disease.

In many countries, particularly developing ones, workers often live in communities near their workplaces or in rapidly urbanizing environments. Lack of safe drinking water and of access to sanitation services, and pollution from transportation, factories and industrial complexes, can place an additional burden on workers' health, partly due to the degraded quality of basic environmental services such as clean air, water and soil. Measures to ensure healthy workplace environments have positive impacts on the health and safety of workers. However, if a healthy environment is not ensured for day-to-day living, human health is still compromised.

Increasingly, policy-makers are recognizing the many ways in which changing economic, social, political and institutional driving forces impact human health and health services. The drivers range from the pressures of a globalized economy to the mandates of negotiated international treaties and the possibilities created by fast-changing technologies. In this dynamic landscape, focusing solely on technical improvements in the efficiency, breadth or capacity of health systems needs to be re-examined. Cross-sectoral linkages between health and the environment can provide valuable information for policy- and decision-makers.

While information provision is necessary, often it will not change practices on the ground. To influence and convince decision-makers, it is essential to demonstrate that cross-sectoral partnerships make sound economic sense. Using the tools of economic evaluation to address health and environmental problems can create additional synergies. It enables health policy-makers to maximize opportunities for health promotion and protection, and to negotiate beneficial policies with other decision-makers.

One of the most important criteria that policy-makers consider when they choose strategic interventions is the cost-benefit profile of various options. Economic analysis helps decision-makers measure *efficiency* – either reaching a defined health and environmental goal with the lowest financial cost, or (alternatively) obtaining the highest level of benefits from a defined level of resources. From a workplace perspective, better identification of the quantitative links between health and environment can help reduce risks to workers and their communities.

The impact of the environment on workers' health

Improving the health of workers requires the planning and delivery of comprehensive programmes which address all the major determinants. Such programmes consist of:

❑ *Occupational health services,* such as prevention of workplace health and safety risks to health and safety, occupational diseases and injuries, promotion of workers' health (e.g. providing a smoke-free environment or improving employees' physical fitness);
❑ *Basic health services,* i.e. provision of primary health care and control of certain communicable diseases (e.g. malaria, HIV/AIDS, avian flu, SARS, viral hepatitis, tuberculosis) at the workplace (Box 3.3.2); and

---

Box 3.3.2

Costa Rica: A trade union campaign against discrimination because of HIV/AIDS[73]

For some HIV positive workers, discrimination can actually be more deadly than the disease itself. In Costa Rica, the Central de Trabajadores Rerum Novarum (CTRN) has conducted an anti-discrimination campaign on behalf of these workers. It aims at forging an alliance of labour organizations, NGOs and governments in a number of Central American countries. The consultation process has taken place in Costa Rica, Dominican Republic, Guatemala, Haiti, Honduras, Nicaragua, Panama and El Salvador.

The campaign has assessed the status of HIV/AIDS in the workplace, devised strategies and built alliances. It has also developed a methodology for analyzing strategies, and promoted cooperation between trade union organizations, NGOs working on HIV/AIDS, governments and employers in implementing strategies and future actions to prevent HIV/AIDS at the workplace and to assist related activities. A key component of this work has involved promoting awareness and training trade union leaders, who were often ill-informed.

As a result of the campaign, labour organizations are better informed about the disease and can help ensure adequate understanding in the workplace and appropriate treatment of those affected. HIV/AIDS has also come to figure on the agenda of participating organizations.

Most of the countries involved now provide HIV/AIDS testing. All have signed cooperation agreements and defined priorities for action among organizations.

---

73 Based on the case study presented by Rodrigo Villalta, representing Central de Trabajadores Rerum Novarum (CTRN), at the Trade Union Assembly on Labour and the Environment / WILL 2006 in Nairobi.

❏ *Environmental health services* to prevent negative health impacts associated with the work site on the neighbouring population (very often workers and their families) and to ensure access to safe water and sanitation at the workplace.[74]

As shown in Figure 3.3.1, improving the health of workers can be viewed in the social-ecological context of the workplace.

Figure 3.3.1

Social-ecological model of the workplace

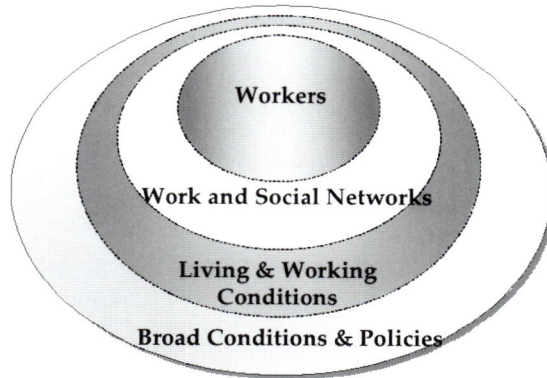

WHO is developing global guidelines and providing assistance in addressing certain priority occupational risks, such as chemicals and psychosocial factors at the workplace. It also works with countries and civil society to improve the control of occupational and work-related diseases (e.g. prevention of occupational cancer and silicosis) in cooperation with ILO. In addition WHO provides guidance and support with respect to defining basic workplace health protection criteria and improving the coverage of basic occupational health services.

At the World Summit on Sustainable Development in 2002, the people of the world asked WHO to strengthen and promote its programme to reduce occupational deaths, injuries and illnesses, and to link occupational health with the promotion of public health.[75] In response, WHO launched the development of a Global Plan of Action on Workers' Health to attain the objectives of the Global Strategy on Occupational Health for All (WHO 1994). This plan will focus on developing healthy workplaces, strengthening the performance of health systems in regard to workers' health, and reducing health inequalities at workplaces. It will also deal with addressing workers' health issues through non-health policies, such as those on employment, sustainable development and environmental protection. For example, there is a need to better integrate concerns about the health of workers into the environmental and social impact assessments of future economic development projects, and to address workers' health in climate adaptation policies and programmes.

---

74 "Environmental health comprises those aspects of human health, including quality of life, that are determined by physical, chemical, biological, social, and psychosocial factors in the environment. It also refers to the theory and practice of assessing, correcting, controlling, and preventing those factors in the environment that can potentially affect adversely the health of present and future generations." Definition from the WHO Public Health and Environment (PHE) web page (www.who.int/phe/en/).

75 Johannesburg Plan of Implementation, VI. Health and sustainable development, Article 46 (m) (www.un.org/esa/sustdev/documents/WSSD_POI_PD/English/POIToc.htm).

Furthermore, a number of ILO standards have been developed to protect workers with respect to both specific risks and specific sectors. These standards are often those most likely to have an improving effect on the environment.

Health and environment of workers in the context of globalization

One of the biggest challenges facing the world of work today is globalization. The International Monetary Fund defines globalization as "a historical process, the result of human innovation and technological progress. It refers to the increasing integration of economies around the world, particularly through trade and financial flows. The term sometimes also refers to the movement of people (labour) and knowledge (technology) across international borders" (IMF 2002).

The evolution of globalization has not resulted in an equitable distribution of benefits, particularly in developing countries. Trade, financial, economic and environmental policies need to be looked at holistically to ensure that the benefits of globalization have a broad reach and do not unduly impact on workers, including on their health.

One-third of trade disputes between countries are on the grounds of health. Therefore, health can be a powerful argument for mobilizing global trade mechanisms to protect workers and their communities. It might be possible, for example, to use trade mechanisms to improve both workers' health and the environment by eliminating technical barriers to trade in protective equipment, and by removing subsidies for hazardous productions or industries. Other tools include restricting trade in hazardous industrial and agricultural products (e.g. asbestos), unsafe technologies and hazardous wastes.

The Basel Convention establishes a mechanism to govern transboundary movements of hazardous wastes, including monitoring of international trade in these wastes, prevention of illegal trade in them, and export and import licensing systems. Incorporating workers' health and environmentally related issues in global trade would require introducing global standards for basic workplace health and environmental protection and strengthening countries' capacities to assess the health and environmental impacts of bilateral and multilateral trade agreements. It would also require enforcing occupational and public health legislation based on international law. In addition, it would be necessary to establish a global observatory to identify cases of double standards and the transfer of risks and hazardous technologies.

In summary, health can be a powerful argument for reaching agreements and mobilizing action, in partnership between the labour and environmental sectors. Global processes represent both challenges and opportunities for improving workers' health and the environment. Trade unions can be agents of change for promoting a culture of life, health and safety in the world of work.

Common concerns, common solutions

As demonstrated by the asbestos case (Box 3.3.3), there are a number of relationships between environmental, public health and economic policies and agendas. Such relationships are increasingly being acknowledged. They should be taken into consideration in framing policies and actions on occupational health and safety and on environmental protection.

Synchronies can be established between actions taken at the workplace and those taken to protect the general environment. This need is illustrated by the fact that, in many multinational companies, occupational health and safety programmes are organized and implemented together with programmes for environmental protection.

Box 3.3.3

Asbestos: an international challenge

Continuous use of asbestos is a cause of great concern in the world today. Despite a reduction in asbestos production from over 5 million tonnes during the 1970s and 1980s to 2 million tonnes today, asbestos use is actually growing in developing countries. Preventive safety and health facilities in these countries are largely underdeveloped, while exposure levels are high. Extensive use of asbestos in industrialized countries in the past has resulted in a well-documented asbestos epidemic today. According to an ILO estimate, there are 100 000 deaths every year from lung cancer and mesothelioma caused by previous exposures to asbestos. This figure does not take into account the thousands of people disabled or killed by asbestosis, an incurable disease.

The total number of workers and communities exposed to asbestos in the past is unknown but very significant. Millions of new victims are expected to be severely affected in future. The report of the Annual Congress of the European Respiratory Society in 2001 indicates that "one in seven people in western societies may have been adversely affected by exposure to asbestos."

Figures for projected deaths are high and can be correlated with increasing asbestos use in the past, which reached its peak in the 1980s. For example, 200 000 deaths from mesothelioma may be expected in the period 1995-2029 in just six European countries (France, Germany, Italy, the Netherlands, Switzerland and the UK). It is possible that these may be closely correlated with the quantities of asbestos imported into these countries. If extrapolated to the whole of Western Europe, with added lung cancer deaths, the number of deaths may be as high as 500 000. This also demonstrates the magnitude of harmful exposures to asbestos and the probability of significant morbidity and mortality resulting from these exposures in the future.

Asbestos use is also an environmental and public health concern. Thousands of tonnes of asbestos remain in buildings and need to be removed. This will produce huge amounts of asbestos waste, posing a serious problem with respect to disposal and environmental risks. Asbestos disposed to landfill keeps its carcinogenic properties.

There are significant public health concerns, as members of workers' families and people who live near production sites are at risk. There are cases of asbestos-related diseases being diagnosed among family members who were exposed to clothes contaminated with asbestos. In general, workers' knowledge about health risks due to asbestos exposure is low. Many do not mention such exposure in their work history at the time the diagnosis of asbestos-related diseases is made.

In addition to huge human suffering and deaths, asbestos use results in a serious strain on national compensation systems and economic losses for enterprises. France, for example, is expected to spend 27-37 billion euros in the next 20 years to compensate victims of asbestos-related diseases. Moreover, there is an asbestos litigation crisis. In the United States more than 600 000 people have filed legal claims and more than 8 400 companies have been named as defendants. Sixty-seven companies have been forced into bankruptcy, with the loss of thousands of jobs. US insurers and companies agreed in 2003 to contribute jointly to a US$114 billion compensation fund. This was US$40 billion below the figure established during debates on a bill sponsored by US Senator Orrin Hatch, and the deal was criticized by US trade unions. "The terms of this agreement come nowhere close to covering the costs of expected disease claims," said John Sweeney, President of the trade union federation AFL-CIO. [76]

Millions of workers in developing countries continue to be unnecessarily exposed to asbestos, despite the fact that it is a carcinogen. Chrysotile asbestos, which accounts for 95 per cent of today's asbestos production and use, is classified as a carcinogen by the WHO International Agency for Research on Cancer (IARC).

---

76 Statement by AFL-CIO President John J. Sweeney on Asbestos Defendants' and Insurers' Funding Agreement, 17 October 2003 (www.aflcio.org).

Box 3.3.3 (...cont'd)

The 1998 Classification of the American Conference of Governmental Industrial Hygienists (ACGIH) describes chrysotile asbestos as carcinogen based on its review of scientific literature. The experts who reviewed the ILO/WHO/UNEP International Chemical Safety Cards on chrysotile asbestos in 1999 saw no reason to modify the IARC evaluation, which assigns it to Group 1 as an "agent carcinogenic to humans". Chrysotile asbestos also appears on many national lists of carcinogenic substances. As it is a carcinogen by nature, chrysotile asbestos cannot be harmless. No scientific evidence establishes a level of exposure to chrysotile asbestos below which health risks cease to exist. On the contrary, there are studies showing that the strictest occupational exposure limits in the world for chrysotile asbestos (0.1 f/cc) are estimated to be associated with lifetime risks of 5/1 000 for lung cancer and 2/1 000 for asbestosis. These exposure limits, while technically achievable in a limited number of highly industrialized countries, still result in unacceptable residual health risks. Exposures are often much higher in developing countries, presenting an increased potential for a far greater epidemic of asbestos-related diseases than that seen currently in countries with mature economies.

To date, about 40 countries have taken a principal decision to prohibit the production and use of asbestos, which is completely in line with an occupational safety and health approach to preventive strategy for carcinogenic substances. A ban on asbestos production and use is enforced in the 25 EU Member States. The Global Unions are conducting active campaigns to severely restrict and prohibit asbestos use in countries where this use continues. In 2006 there were numerous activities aimed at promoting a global asbestos ban campaign on the occasion of the 28 April International Commemoration Day for Dead and Injured Workers. Measures also include joint ILO and WHO efforts and the promotion of ILO international instruments such as the ILO Convention on Safety in the Use of Asbestos (ILO 1986), the ILO Occupational Cancer Convention (ILO 1974) and relevant Codes of Practice.

The ILO international instruments provide solid legislative and practical bases for worker protection against harmful asbestos exposures by prescribing comprehensive preventive measures at national and enterprise levels. Among other measures, the ILO Convention on Safety in the Use of Asbestos (28 ratifications) provides for "replacement of asbestos or certain types of asbestos or products containing asbestos by other materials or products ... scientifically evaluated by the competent authorities as harmless or less harmful" [Article 10 (a)]. The ILO Occupational Cancer Convention (35 ratifications) prescribes that "Each Member ... shall make every effort to have carcinogenic substances and agents to which workers may be exposed in the course of their work replaced by non-carcinogenic substances or agents or by less harmful substances or agents; in the choice of substitute substances or agents account shall be taken of their carcinogenic, toxic and other properties" [Article 2 (1)]. It is in line with these provisions that countries tend to introduce alternatives to chrysotile asbestos, along with the development of materials science and new products.

ILO is actively promoting the ratification and voluntary application of its international instruments to improve the efficacy of preventive measures against health risks posed by uses of asbestos and its products, with the active involvement of international and national workers' organizations. It is using all available means, including advocacy campaigns, knowledge management, development of inspection systems and technical co-operation. The important task of building efficient national safety and health systems for worker – and community – protection is formulated straightforwardly in the ILO 2003 Global Strategy on Occupational Safety and Health (ILO 2003) and the ILO Convention on the Promotional Framework for Occupational Safety and Health adopted in June 2006 (ILO 2006a).

More recently, this task of universal elimination of asbestos use has been given higher priority and received new impetus for implementation throughout the world. The International Labour Conference adopted at its 95th Session (June 2006) a Resolution Concerning Asbestos.

Box 3.3.3 (...cont'd)

The Resolution declares that the elimination of the future use of asbestos, and the identification and proper management of asbestos currently in place, are the most effective means to protect workers from asbestos exposure and to prevent future asbestos-related diseases and deaths (ILO 2006b). It also resolves that the ILO Convention on Safety in the Use of Asbestos should not be used to provide justification for, or endorsement of, continued use of asbestos.

To accomplish this challenging task, a strong alliance and concerted actions by all relevant organizations and professionals are required in order to successfully prevent health risks posed by dangerous asbestos exposures through wide international co-operation and effective tripartite activities at national and enterprise levels. These activities would be aimed at the elimination of asbestos-related diseases worldwide.

References

- ILO (International Labour Organization) (1974). Convention No. 139 concerning Prevention and Control of Occupational Hazards caused by Carcinogenic Substances and Agents (www.ilo.org/ilolex/english/convdisp1.htm).

- (1986). Convention No. 162 concerning Safety in the Use of Asbestos (www.ilo.org/ilolex/english/convdisp1.htm).

- (2003). Global Strategy on Occupational Safety and Health (www.ilo.org/public/english/protection/safework/globstrat_e.pdf).

— (2005) Introductory Report: Decent Work – Safe Work. 17th World Congress on Safety and Health in Work (2005) (www.ilo.org/public/english/protection/safework/wdcongrs17/intrep.pdf)

- (2006a). Convention No. 187 concerning the Promotional Framework for Occupational Safety and Health (www.ilo.org/ilolex/english/convdisp1.htm).

- (2006b). Follow-up to resolutions adopted by the 95th Session (2006) of the International Labour Conference and other matters arising: Resolution concerning asbestos (www.ilo.org/public/english/standards/relm/gb/docs/gb297/pdf/gb-3-1.pdf).

- IMF (International Monetary Fund) (2002). Globalization: Threat or Opportunity? (www.imf.org/external/np/exr/ib/2000/041200.htm#I).

- WHO (World Health Organization) (1948). Constitution of the World Health Organization www.searo.who.int/LinkFiles/About_SEARO_const.pdf.).

- (1994). Global Strategy on Occupational Health for All: The Way to Health at Work (www.who.int/occupational_health/globstrategy/en)

- (2002). The World Health Report 2002 - Reducing Risks, Promoting Healthy Life (http://www.who.int/whr/2002/en/).

— (2006). Ecosystems and Human Well-being: Health Synthesis (www.who.int/globalchange/ecosystems/ecosystems05/en/index.html)

3.4. Chemical risks and hazardous substances in the workplace

Tony Musu, Health and Safety Department, European Trade Union Institute for Research, Education and Health and Safety (ETUI-REHS), European Trade Union Confederation (ETUC)

Production of chemical substances worldwide has risen from one million tonnes in 1930 to more than 400 million tonnes today. Tens of thousands of different substances on the world market are used to make virtually every man-made product. Chemicals have contributed to the improvement of living conditions, and there is no denying that they yield benefits which modern society could not do without (e.g. in the production of food and pharmaceuticals). The global chemical industry also contributes to economic prosperity in terms of trade and jobs. Its annual sales are estimated at more than US$1 600 billion. The industry employs over 10 million people worldwide.[77]

However, some chemicals may cause irreversible damage to human health and the environment (Table 3.4.1, Box 3.4.1). In particular, both the manufacture and use of chemicals takes a heavy toll on workers. Millions of them are exposed to chemicals on a daily basis, not only in the chemical industry but also in sectors where they are used, including agriculture, the building trade, the woodworking industry, and automobile, textile and electronics manufacturing.[78]

© *P. Van Peenen / UNEP*

Chemical weapons dump, Canada: *Hazardous chemicals can persist in the environment for decades, accumulating in the food chain, and can be transported far from the original source. They form major health risks for workers, damage the nervous and immune systems, cause cancers and reproductive disorders, and interfere with child development. To save lives and protect the environment by eliminating the most toxic chemicals will cost billions of dollars.*

Chemical hazards are currently a major cause of mortality related to working conditions in the world. The ILO estimates the annual average number of deaths attributable to occupational exposure to hazardous substances at approximately 440 000 (or 20 per cent of all work-related fatalities).[79] Lung cancers and mesothelioma due to previous asbestos exposure are the main causes with over 160 000 deaths.[80]

---

77   www.icca-chem.org.
78   Including the disassembly of mobile telephones, computers and other electronic equipment, which are often sent from industrialized to developing countries for this purpose. Ship breaking is another example of the transfer of disassembly to developing countries (e.g. India), with potentially lethal consequences for the health of those engaged in this type of work.
79   www.ilo.org/public/english/protection/safework/wdcongrs17/intrep.pdf.
80   See Chapter 3, section 3, "Occupational, environmental and public health" by Ivan D. Ivan, Igor Fedotov and Monica Wehrle-MacDevette.

The ILO also estimates at 160 million the annual number of non-fatal, work-related diseases in the world's workforce of 2.8 billion people. No data are available on the percentage of occupational diseases related to chemicals exposure at global level. Nevertheless, according to a calculation based on Eurostat data, up to 30 per cent of all occupational diseases recognized annually in Europe can be ascribed to exposure to hazardous chemicals. These work-related diseases include cancers, disorders of the nervous system, respiratory diseases and skin diseases.[81]

Table 3.4.1

Estimated percentage of occupational diseases related to exposure to chemical substances in Europe

Type of occupational disease	Estimated % of cases related to exposure to chemicals	Proportion of all recognized occupational diseases‡	Estimated % of recognized occupational diseases related to exposure to chemicals
Cancers	4-90%*	5%	0.2-4.5%*
Neurological disorders	2%	8%	0.2%
Respiratory diseases	36-89%*	14%	5-12.5*%
Skin diseases	88%	14%	12.3%
Total			**~ 18 to 30%***

* Including chemical dust like asbestos or crystalline silica
‡ Source: Eurostat EODS data, 2004
Source: T. Musu, REACHing the workplace, 2004.

One of the main factors explaining this situation is lack of knowledge about the inherent hazardous properties of most chemicals found on the market and their sound and safe use. It is an appalling fact that over 99 per cent of the total volume of marketed substances have not undergone any in-depth assessment of their risks to human health and the environment.[82] The direct consequence of this lack of data is that many hazardous chemicals are not classified as such, and are therefore sold without appropriate labels or safety data sheets. Many chemicals are thus used in the workplace even though we do not know precisely (or only too late) what effects they might have on the health of workers exposed to them.

Chemical risks at work derive both from the intrinsic hazardous properties of chemicals and from workers' levels of exposure to these substances, reflecting the way in which they are used in the workplace (Box 2.1.4). When it comes to safe use of chemicals at work, the situation varies according to countries, sectors of activity and company size. In industrialized countries, even if important improvements have still to be made in big companies, the problems lie mainly with small and medium-sized enterprises (SMEs), where existing legislation or good practices aimed at protecting workers' health from chemical risks are scarcely enforced.

---

81 www.europa.eu.int/comm/eurostat.
82 Strategy for a future Chemicals Policy, White Paper, COM(2001)88 final, European Commission, 27 February 2001.

Box 3.4.1

Examples of chemicals that may damage or impair the environment and human health

Bioaccumulated chemicals: Chemicals accumulate in living things when they are taken up and stored faster than they are broken down (i.e. metabolized) or excreted. Bioaccumulation is a normal process. Over time, it increases the concentrations of a chemical in a biological organism, compared with its environmental concentrations. Bioaccumulation only has adverse effects when the equilibrium between exposure and inoculation is overwhelmed, relative to the harmfulness of the chemical in question. (Related terms are "bioconcentration" and "biomagnification").

Biocides: Synthetic or natural chemicals (e.g. herbicides, insecticides, rodenticides) that are toxic to organisms. European Community legislation distinguishes between "plant protection products" and "biocidal products".

Chlorofluroocarbons (CFCs): Compounds of fluorine and chlorine used as propellants in aerosol cans, in the manufacture of plastic foam boxes, as a refrigerant, and as a cleaner of circuit boards for computers. They have been widely banned, and substitutes have been developed, since in the atmosphere they break down into chlorine atoms which destroy the ozone layer.

Chlorinated hydrocarbons (CHCs): Compounds that contain chlorine, carbon and hydrogen. This term is used to describe organochlorine pesticides (e.g. lindane and DDT), industrial chemicals (e.g. PCBs) and chlorine waste products (e.g. dioxins and furans).

Dioxins: Toxic (and probably carcinogenic) chemical family. Dioxins are widely distributed in the environment, and are persistent and bioaccumulated. Many people today have detectable levels of dioxins in their tissues.

Endocrine disruptors: Chemicals that can disrupt endocrine systems, which results in developmental and reproductive problems. There are concerns that endocrine disruptors in the environment threaten both humans and wildlife.

Heavy metals: Metallic elements (e.g. mercury, arsenic and lead) that are toxic and poisonous at low concentrations. Not only are they dangerous individually, but they tend to **bioaccumulate** (see above).

Hydrofluorocarbons (HFCs): Compounds that contain fluorine, carbon and hydrogen. Some HFCs have been considered by scientists and industry as acceptable alternatives to chloroflurorocarbons (CFCs) and hydrochlorofluorocarbons (HCFCs) since they do not contain chlorine and therefore do not directly affect stratospheric ozone. Nevertheless, they have other harmful environmental effects.

Persistent chemicals: The longer chemicals persist in the environment in an unchanged form, the greater the potential for human and environmental exposure to them. Usually, persistence is measured or estimated in regard to air, water, soil or sediment.

Polychlorinated biphenyls (PCBs): Toxic, possibly carcinogenic compounds used as coolants and lubricants. PCBs are not readily broken down in the environment. In countries where they have been banned, in some cases since the 1970s, they continue to be released to air, water and soil. PCBs can only be destroyed by special incinerators at extremely high temperature.

Persistent organic pollutants (POPs): Substances that persist in the environment, bioaccumulate through the food web, and present a risk of adverse effects to human health and the environment. There is evidence of long-range transport of Pops to regions where they have never been used or produced.

Polychlorinated biphenyls (PCBs): Persistent organic pollutants and have entered the environment through both use and disposal. They were used in hundreds of industrial and commercial applications (electrical equipment, paints, plastics) before being banned in the 1970s, when it was discovered that they accumulated in the environment and were toxic to human.

> ### Box 3.4.1 (...cont'd)
>
> **Stable substances**: Substances that are not easily decomposed or otherwise modified chemically.
>
> Among many other well-known examples of widely used chemicals which can damage human health and the environment should be mentioned organochlorine pesticides, brominated flame retardants, and benzene, an industrial solvent.

Generally speaking, the situation in developing countries is particularly bad. Often chemicals are used at industrial and agricultural sites with highly toxic active ingredients which, although they may be banned in industrialized countries, are still marketed in the developing world. Protective equipment is often not available, and information and training are mostly lacking. Due to less stringent regulations and (as a consequence) deliberate corporate strategies to relocate production to countries with lower standards, workers in these countries are increasingly becoming victims of social, environmental and health and safety dumping.

The role of trade unions

Trade unions are major actors in shaping and defending workers' rights, including health and safety at work. They are willing to participate in any chemical risk prevention programme, and they must be involved in urgent action to ensure sound and safe use of chemicals within enterprises, as well as on a national, regional and international level.

Since only a sustainable chemical industry will be competitive on a medium to long-term basis in a society that increasingly demands stricter environmental and health standards, the chemical industry will have to modernize. Safer and cleaner alternatives must be created through substitution of highly hazardous substances, transformation of processes, and product innovation. Where these changes may have negative social repercussions, companies and national authorities must provide the necessary instruments for a just transition. Collective bargaining with employers should therefore not only aim at ensuring that workers are given sufficient information and training to perform their work in a safe and healthy way, but should also be used to make corporate social responsibility a reality. Certain key notions that trade unions have insisted on for decades must be put into practice: e.g. the precautionary principle, the substitution principle, cleaner production, and best available technique.

Voluntary initiatives such as "responsible care" and "product stewardship" need to be encouraged. However, such agreements and initiatives are not enough by themselves to ensure production and use of chemicals with a sufficient level of safety. Trade unions do not consider them as alternatives, but rather as complement to legislation.

At national level, trade unions can campaign for policy-makers to set up or improve legislation aimed at managing chemical risks and protecting the health of workers exposed to hazardous substances. Equally important is the existence of efficient health care systems to identify, treat and monitor cases of chemical accidents, poisoning and workplace illnesses. National governments can also be called upon to ratify and apply ILO conventions that set proper conditions for dealing with chemical risks effectively. These are conventions covering the use and management of chemicals,[83] workers' rights[84] and

---

83 ILO Conventions No. 170 (safety in the use of chemicals), No. 174 (industrial accidents) and No. 162 (protection against asbestos).
84 ILO Conventions No. 81 (labour inspection), No. 121 (employment injury) and No. 161 (occupational health services).

child labour.[85] Implementation of global conventions on the management of highly toxic chemicals, including certain pesticides, from production to disposal stages is also critical. These include: the Stockholm Convention on Persistent Organic Pollutants, the Rotterdam Convention on the Prior Informed Consent Procedure for Certain Hazardous Chemicals in International Trade, and the Basel Convention on the Control of Transboundary Movements of Hazardous Waste and their Disposal.

All countries should implement the new globally harmonized system (GHS) for the classification and labelling of chemicals adopted at UN level.[86] This is crucial to ensure that information on physical hazards and toxicity from chemicals is available, in order to enhance the protection of workers, consumers and the environment during the handling, transport and use of these chemicals.

Besides the different actions trade unions can undertake at company or national level to promote the safe use of chemicals, workers and their representatives have also an important role to play at global and regional level.

Dealing with chemical risks at the global level

Given the global nature of chemical risks and the effects of globalization, there is increasing recognition of the importance of sound management of chemicals at international level. The 2002 World Summit on Sustainable Development agreed to take action such that by 2020 chemical substances would be used and produced in ways that lead to the minimization of significant "adverse effects on human health and the environment".[87]

For this reason, trade unions have collaborated in efforts to implement the Strategic Approach to International Chemicals Management (SAICM), in order to produce a policy framework for international action on chemical hazards.[88] Adopted by the International Conference on Chemicals Management (ICCM) in Dubai on 6 February 2006, SAICM contains valuable principles and actions for the sound management of chemicals at the global level. Of particular importance for trade unions, SAICM will help close gaps and address discrepancies in the capacity to achieve sustainable chemicals management between developed countries on the one hand and developing countries and countries with economies in transition on the other. Cooperation is also needed, however, between local unions in developing countries and trade unions in developed countries, in order to safeguard decent work and prevent dumping practices from occurring.

Another way in which trade unions can help achieve important objectives in regard to chemical risk prevention at global level is the organization of a worldwide campaign to ban carcinogenic substances like asbestos. In June 2005, the Global Unions kicked off a campaign for a worldwide ban on the production and use of asbestos. Since the launch an extensive lobby has been carried out. The Global Unions have contacted the labour, environmental and health ministries of every government with a request to ban asbestos in their own country (if it has not already been banned) and to join the campaign for a global ban. Governments have also been asked to promote employment transition measures to protect workers who would be displaced by such a ban. Campaign organizers, backed by ILO and WHO, are confident that there is no turning back now and that they will achieve a global ban (no matter how long it takes).

---

85 ILO Convention No. 182.
86 www.unece.org/trans/danger/publi/ghs/ghs_welcome_e.html.
87 www.johannesburgsummit.org.
88 www.chem.unep.ch/saicm.

Dealing with chemical risks at European level

Europe is undertaking a complete and radical review of its chemical substances policy because the EU legislation in place has not been operating effectively enough and is incapable of safeguarding the health of workers and consumers or protecting the environment. This reform sets up a comprehensive system for the Registration, Evaluation and Authorization of Chemicals (REACH). Its principal aspect lies in the principle of shifting the burden of proof from regulatory authorities to the chemical industry.

Under the proposed REACH system, companies manufacturing or importing chemical substances in quantities of one tonne or more per year will be required, prior to placing them on the market, to register such substances in order to demonstrate that they can be used safely. In addition, authorization will be required for highly hazardous substances like CMRs (carcinogenic, mutagenic or toxic to reproduction), PBTs (persistent, bioaccumulative and toxic), vPvBs (very persistent and very bio-accumulative) and other substances with serious and irreversible effects on humans and the environment

The European trade unions have supported REACH strongly since this reform was proposed in 2001 (Box 3.4.2).First, they believe that producers and downstream users of chemical substances should be responsible for all safety-related aspects of their products with respect to that part of the life-cycle in which they are involved (including recycling and disposal). They welcome the adoption of both the principle of shifting the burden of proof and the "no data, no market" principle.

Second, trade unions are convinced that REACH will boost the protection of workers exposed to chemicals by supplying missing information on safe uses and by improving their communication along the entire production chain. In a study commissioned from the University of Sheffield by trade unions, it is demonstrated that in Europe REACH would help avoid 50 000 cases of occupational respiratory diseases and 40 000 cases of occupational skin diseases per year due to exposure to dangerous chemicals. That would add up to total average savings of 3.5 billion euros over 10 years within the EU-25, an amount approximately equivalent to the total costs of REACH for the European chemical industry.

Third, trade unions consider that REACH and its authorization procedures will promote the application of the substitution principle for substances of very high concern. The new EU policy presents a real opportunity to foster innovation and employment in the industry by encouraging it to develop new chemicals that will be less harmful to workers, consumers and the environment.

The REACH Regulation was formally adopted on 18 December 2006 by the Council of Environment Ministers, following the vote in second reading of the European Parliament on 13 December 2006. REACH will enter into force on 1 June 2007.[89] European trade unions will continue to monitor the REACH process and to do their utmost to ensure that REACH contributes to the creation of a more socially responsible Europe. To meet the requirements set out in Johannesburg in 2002, they also demand that the principles of REACH be recognized worldwide, thereby ensuring fair conditions for global competition.

---

89 The text of the Regulation was published on 30 December 2006 in the Official Journal of the European Union L 396 (http://ec.europa.eu/environment/chemicals/reach/reach_intro.htm).

Conclusions

Trade unions are central actors in the proper management of chemicals. They have a role to play, from the local (in enterprises) to the global level, including at national and regional levels. To play this role effectively, trade unions must have the possibility and the ability to do so. This means that their input must be recognized and codified, and that they must build their capacities. This can be done through the ratification of ILO conventions and the elaboration of fundamental social standards within the ILO. Strengthening trade union competencies can be achieved through learning by doing, increased exchange of information and experiences between unions, and better cooperation and co-ordination with NGOs.

Governments and enterprises must be convinced that preventing chemical risks at the workplace not only benefits companies and their workers, but also public health and the environment. Cleaner production and safe use of chemicals can be achieved provided that all workplace parties understand and exercise the will to balance social, economic and environmental objectives.

Box 3.4.2

ETUC's REACH Campaign[90]

The European Trade Union Confederation (ETUC) initiated a campaign to promote the proposed European Union regulatory framework for the Registration, Evaluation and Authorization of Chemicals (REACH), designed to replace existing European legislation with a single management system for chemical substances. The cornerstone of the regulation was that the burden of proof lay with industry, which would have to demonstrate that registered chemicals could be used safely.

ETUC undertook a number of initiatives to promote the new system of chemicals management, including setting up a working group to define the trade union position on the new legislation, preparing an explanatory booklet for workers and performing its own impact study. In addition, it organized a conference in March 2005 involving a wide range of political, civil society and other stakeholders, with the objective of presenting trade union proposals for improving REACH.

As a result of ETUC's REACH campaign of ETUC, workers became major actors in the debate, and the text approved by the European Parliament meets a number of key ETUC recommendations. ETUC will continue to monitor REACH to ensure that it contributes to workers' health and the sustainable management of chemicals.

90 Based on the case study presented by the author, representing the European Trade Union Confederation (ETUC), at the Trade Union Assembly on Labour and the Environment / WILL 2006.

References

- Musu, Tony (2004). REACHing the workplace,

- European Trade Union Confederation (ETUC) (www.etuc.org)

- European Union REACH home page (http://ec.europa.eu/environment/chemicals/reach/reach_intro.htm)

- UNEP Chemicals (www.chem.unep.ch).

- UNEP Division of Industry, Technology and Economics (UNEP DTIE) (2004) Managing the risks of chemicals. Special issue of Industry and environment, UNEP DTIE's quarterly review (www.uneptie.org; www.uneptie.org/media/review/ie_home.htm).

4. A Common Framework for Action: A Time to Act

Adriana Zacarias Farah, *Division of Technology, Industry and Economics, United Nations Environment Programme*

© S. Compoint / UNEP

Capping an oil well, Kuwait: *Air pollution from oil well fires creates serious health hazards as the smoke contains mercury, sulphur, nitrogen, dioxins and furans. Oil spills seep into the ground and contaminate fragile desert ecosystems. Ninety per cent of the world's transport depends on oil. To mitigate climate change by cutting emissions of the main greenhouse gas, carbon dioxide, would mean burning far less oil than we do today.*

4.1. Towards sustainable consumption and production patterns

In the 21st century the world population is expected to reach 9 billion and total world output is expected to quadruple. Global environmental trends continue to present grave challenges and threats, as underlined by figures in UNEP's third *Global Environment Outlook* report, *GEO-3* (UNEP 2002).[91] Use of natural resources, and levels of pollution and waste, continue to grow despite gains in cleaner production and eco-efficiency. Global use of fossil fuels (coal, petroleum and natural gas) was almost five times higher in 2002 than in 1950.[92] Carbon dioxide levels in the atmosphere in 2002 were 18 per cent higher than in 1960; they are estimated to be over 30 per cent higher today than at the beginning of the Industrial Revolution in the mid 18th century. About half the world's original forest cover has disappeared, while another 30 per cent is degraded or fragmented. In 1999 global use of wood for fuel, lumber, paper and other products was more than twice that in 1950 (Worldwatch Institute 2004, 2005a, b). Unless we decouple economic growth from environmental degradation, modern societies will simply not be able to sustain their current quality of life.

Nevertheless, some positive changes are taking place. For example, consumers are increasingly interested in the world that lies beyond the products they buy. Apart from price and quality, they want to know how, where and by whom these products were made. They are also concerned about poverty and labour conditions, as demonstrated by the increasing market share of "fair trade" products.[93]

The growing need for sustainable consumption and production policy

In the last 15 to 20 years, the need for sustainable consumption and production (SCP) policies has increasingly been expressed at the international policy level. For example:

❏ The Declaration on Environment and Development, adopted at the UN Conference on Environment and Development (UNCED) in Rio de Janeiro in 1992, called upon countries to change their unsustainable production and consumption patterns in order to achieve sustainable development and a higher quality of life for all people;[94]

❏ Chapter 4 of Agenda 21 ("Changing Consumption Patterns"), also adopted in Rio in 1992, is dedicated to sustainable consumption and production;[95]

---

91   See the Introduction by Fatou Ndoye.

92   At the beginning of the 21st century, over three-quarters of the world's energy was being supplied by fossil fuels, mainly coal, petroleum and natural gas. While fossil fuel consumption has grown enormously since the Second World War, the relative shares of coal, petroleum and natural gas have changed. Almost two-thirds of the fossil fuel consumed in 1950 was coal, but coal's share was less than one-third by the end of the 1990s (roughly equivalent to that of natural gas). An increasing number of geologists and other experts today doubt that fossil fuel reserves will continue to be adequate to meet rising global demand. Of course, as global fossil fuel consumption rises, so do the (very serious) health and environmental risks of pollution and of climate change (see, for example, section 3.1, "Climate change and energy" by Peter Poschen and Olfa Khazri). Among many other sources on fossil fuel consumption and its consequences, see UNEP 2002; Worldwatch Institute 2004 and 2005a, b.

93   The mission of Fairtrade Labelling Organizations International (FLO), one of the largest fair trade standard setting and certification bodies, is to "enable sustainable development and empowerment of disadvantaged producers and workers in developing countries" (www.fairtrade.net/support_fairtrade.html).

94   Principle 8 is "To achieve sustainable development and a higher quality of life for all people, States should reduce and eliminate unsustainable patterns of production and consumption and promote appropriate demographic policies." (www.unep.org/Documents.multilingual/Default.asp?DocumentID=78&ArticleID=1163).

95   www.un.org/esa/sustdev/documents/agenda21/.

- ❏ The 1999 UN Guidelines for Consumer Protection provide governments with a comprehensive framework for policy-setting to achieve more sustainable consumption and production;[96]
- ❏ Sustainable consumption and production was a top priority on the agenda of the 2002 World Summit on Sustainable Development (WSSD) in Johannesburg. Chapter III of the Johannesburg Plan of Implementation calls for developing a ten-year framework of programmes to accelerate the shift towards sustainable consumption and production patterns, in order to promote social and economic development within ecosystems' carrying capacity by addressing and – where appropriate – delinking economic growth and environmental degradation. This is to be done through improving the efficiency and sustainability of resource use and production processes, and by reducing resource degradation, pollution and waste.[97]

In developing sustainable development and consumption policies, one of the main messages has been that a single instrument will not fix the problem. It will be necessary to design a package of mixed instruments, including regulatory frameworks, economic instruments and voluntary measures. It is also important to actively involve all stakeholders (e.g. governments, industry, business, the advertising profession, consumer associations, academia and, of course, environmental NGOs and trade unions).

Contributing to poverty reduction by promoting sustainable consumption and production is one of UNEP's top priorities. This is especially relevant with respect to developing countries. The world's poor deserve the same quality of life as that enjoyed by the majority of people in developed countries. The essential questions are how to decouple economic growth from environmental degradation, and how to provide poor countries and communities with what they need and want without damaging the earth's life support systems. Promoting sustainable consumption and production also represents a new opportunity to leapfrog to sustainability, thus avoiding repeating the same high-polluting phases of development that industrialized countries have gone through.

SCP is becoming a priority for countries worldwide. It is necessary to look at innovative ways to meet (basic) needs, and to develop new innovative product service systems. This is particularly important when we consider the emerging "global consumer class". Large groups of middle class consumers (e.g. in rapidly developing countries like Brazil, China and India) exhibit increasingly similar consumption patterns.

The Marrakech Process

As a response to the call by the Johannesburg Plan of Implementation, UNEP and the UN Division of Economic and Social Affairs (DESA) have been the leading agencies developing a ten-year framework of programmes (10YFP) on Sustainable Consumption and Production at the global and regional level. This work is being carried out in cooperation with other UN agencies, national governments, donor countries and other stakeholders (i.e. the private sector, consumer councils, environmental NGOs and, to some extent, trade unions).[98]

The first international expert meeting on the ten-year framework took place in Marrakech, Morocco, in June 2003, launching the "Marrakech Process". The Marrakech Process

---

96   www.un.org/esa/sustdev/sdissues/consumption/cpp1225.htm.
97   www.un.org/esa/sustdev/documents/WSSD_POI_PD/English/POIToc.htm.
98   www.unep.fr/pc/sustain/10year/home.htm.

includes regular global and regional meetings, supported by informal expert task forces and roundtables, to promote concrete project implementation and progress on the ten-year SCP framework. The Marrakech meeting identified a number of key priorities, including the development of SCP policies and integration of economic, environmental and social aspects.

Development of the 10YFP consists of the following phases:

❑ Organizing regional consultations to promote awareness of, and identify priorities and needs for, sustainable consumption and production;
❑ Building regional strategies and implementation mechanisms with regional and national ownership;
❑ Implementing concrete projects and programmes on the local, regional and national levels;
❑ Monitoring and evaluating progress.

The UN Commission on Sustainable Development (CSD) will review progress on the 10YFP during its 2010-2011 two-year cycle.[99]

Between 2003 and 2005 nine regional consultations were held in Africa, Asia-Pacific, Europe, and Latin America and the Caribbean. Each region identified its needs and priorities in terms of SCP. Among the most outstanding outcomes of these regional consultations was the development of the African 10-Year Framework of Programmes on SCP, launched in May 2006 in Ethiopia. Latin America has also developed a regional Strategy on SCP and has officially set up the Regional Government Council on SCP, supported by the regional Forum of Environment Ministries. Europe is in the process of developing its Action Plan on Sustainable Consumption and Production, within the European Union's Sustainable Development Strategy.[100]

The Marrakech Task Forces: from strategies to implementation

To support implementation of concrete projects (phase 3 of the 10YFP), and to focus on the specific themes of SCP, the Marrakech Task Forces have been created, with participation by experts from developing and developed countries. The Task Forces are informal groups of countries and organizations that join together to work on a specific SCP issue, committing themselves to carrying out a concrete set of activities which support implementation of concrete projects. There are no specific rules or obligations, as this initiative is purely voluntary. So far, the following task forces have been formed:

❑ Cooperation with Africa (led by Germany);
❑ Sustainable Products (led by the United Kingdom);
❑ Sustainable Lifestyles (led by Sweden);
❑ Sustainable Procurement (led by Switzerland);
❑ Sustainable Tourism (led by France);
❑ Sustainable Building and Construction (led by Finland);
❑ Education for Sustainable Consumption (led by Italy).[101]

---

99 www.un.org/esa/sustdev/csd/policy.htm.
100 For the reports on the Marrakech Regional Consultations, see www.un.org/esa/sustdev/documents/WSSD_POI_PD/ English/POIToc.htm. For the EU Sustainable Development Strategy, see http://ec.europa.eu/environment/eussd/.
101 For more information on the task forces, see www.unep.fr/sustain/10year/taskforce.htm.

Other countries have expressed interest in creating task forces that focus on waste management, SMEs and social issues (including labour conditions and trade unions). The task forces are mainly composed of governments and NGOs. Although trade unions can participate, very few are currently involved. Their involvement should be enhanced.

Cooperation Dialogue: bringing development agencies aboard

Another important implementation mechanism consists in working with regional banks and development agencies. Recognizing the important role of development agencies, the Marrakech Process has initiated a Cooperation Dialogue between these agencies and SCP experts. The Dialogue Session, initiated at the "Marrakech+2" meeting in Costa Rica in September 2005, aims at building better cooperation in the implementation of development projects that promote SCP while contributing to poverty reduction.[102]

The Marrakech Process has emphasized the importance of linking work on SCP with poverty reduction and the attainment of the Millennium Development Goals (MDGs).[103] Sustainable consumption and production policies should also be developed and integrated into national sustainable development strategies and other plans and strategies, including Poverty Reduction Strategy Papers where applicable.[104]

Moreover, adopting a gender perspective is critical to the success of sustainable consumption policies. Men and women have different consumption patterns and attitudes towards greener consumption. In most developed countries, for example, women tend to use public transport more than men. They also have different attitudes towards individual transport and environmentally friendly products, and may respond differently to different messages and incentives when it comes to adopting more sustainable lifestyles.

Sustainable Consumption and Production and trade unions

Chapter III of the Johannesburg Plan of Implementation on "Changing Unsustainable Patterns of Consumption and Production" (see above) calls for actions at all levels to encourage and promote the development of a ten-year framework of programmes "in support of regional and national initiatives to accelerate the shift towards sustainable consumption and production, to promote social and economic development within the carrying capacity of ecosystems and, where appropriate, delinking economic growth and environmental degradation through improving efficiency and sustainability in the use of resources and production processes and reducing resources degradation, pollution and waste."

---

102 For more information on the Marrakech Cooperation Dialogue, see www.unep.fr/pc/sustain/10year/Cooperation%20Dialogue.htm.

103 The Millennium Development Goals (MDGs) were adopted at the UN Millennium Summit in September 2000. They are time-bound, measurable goals and targets for combating poverty, hunger, disease, illiteracy, environmental degradation, and discrimination against women. A wide range of commitments on human rights, good governance and democracy are outlined in the Summit's Millennium Declaration (www.un.org/millenniumgoals/).

104 "Poverty Reduction Strategy Papers (PRSP) are prepared by member countries through a participatory process involving domestic stakeholders as well as external development partners, including the World Bank and International Monetary Fund. Updated every three years with annual progress reports, PRSPs describe the country's macroeconomic, structural and social policies and programmes over a three year or longer horizon to promote broad-based growth and reduce poverty, as well as associated external financing needs and major sources of financing. Interim PRSPs (I-PRSPs) summarize the current knowledge and analysis of a country's poverty situation, describe the existing poverty reduction strategy, and lay out the process for producing a fully developed PRSP in a participatory fashion. The country documents, along with the accompanying IMF/World Bank Joint Staff Assessments (JSAs), are being made available on the World Bank and IMF websites by agreement with the member country as a service to users of the World Bank and IMF websites." Excerpted from the International Monetary Fund (IMF) website (www.imf.org/external/np/prsp/prsp.asp).

Paragraph 18 of Chapter III, on corporate responsibility, implicitly refers to the role of trade unions. It alludes to their potential role in sustainable consumption and production and calls for encouraging "dialogue between enterprises and communities in which they operate and other stakeholders" [paragraph 18(b)]. It also mentions "workplace-based partnerships and programmes, including training and education programmes" [paragraph 18(d)].

In Chapter V, another explicit reference emphasizes the role of the ILO ("Sustainable Development in a Globalizing World"). Paragraph 47(d) calls for supporting the ILO and encouraging "its ongoing work on the social dimension of globalization".

Because of trade unions' dual role as societal forces and lobbying organizations, their activities have traditionally focused on issues that concern the direct interests of union members (e.g. job security, wage levels and working conditions). More recently, trade unions have started to integrate other topics such as education, environmental protection and sustainable development into their agendas.

At the international policy level, the potential role of labour unions in this process is widely acknowledged. Thanks to the growing debate on corporate social and environmental responsibility, unions have begun to rethink the links between societal and workplace issues.

A study conducted for UNEP by Ecologic, *The Role of Labour Unions in the Process Towards Sustainable Consumption and Production* (Heins and others 2004), emphasizes that two crucial developments are currently underway at the international trade union level:

❏ For the first time, trade unions' senior policy level has agreed that sustainable development is a new paradigm for them. This explicit commitment is expected to provide new impetus to the trade union movement;

❏ An as yet unresolved discussion revolves around how sustainability policies should replace (or be combined or integrated with) traditional health and safety issues. While some union representatives have proposed that health and safety could provide the backbone for sustainability at the workplace and beyond, others fear that well-functioning health and safety structures will be weakened if the focus is shifted to sustainable consumption and production.

Due partly to how recent the overall commitment to sustainable development at the international level has been, and partly to the structural characteristics of trade unions in general, progress in implementing approaches is considered to have been slow so far.[105] Although there have been positive advances, as seen in several case studies from around the world, an overall movement still needs to be spurred on.

---

105 See, for example, *Fashioning a New Deal: Workers and Trade Unions at the World Summit for Sustainable Development*, prepared by Global Unions for the WSSD in 2002 (www.icftu.org/www/pdf/reportsouthafricaenglish.pdf).

Box 4.4.1

Sweden: Labelling for an ecological workplace – emissions, energy, ecology and ergonomics[106]

The Swedish Confederation of Professional Employees (TCO) has developed a labelling system, in partnership with NUTEK (the Swedish Agency for Economic and Regional Growth) and the Swedish Nature Conservancy Society.

This project began in the 1980s in response to workers' concerns about emissions from computer screens, and about the safety of working environments generally. Although the government and employers showed no interest, computer manufacturers responded positively to the proposal to establish emissions standards.

The TCO labelling system was introduced in 1992. It was expanded in 1995 to cover economic and ecological standards, including for the working environment of employees involved in production. Today the system's main objective is to provide trade union members with a safer and more ecological workplace through requirements in four categories: emissions, energy, ecology and ergonomics.

As soon as TCO labelling began, results were seen in terms of reduced energy use, lower emissions from electromagnetic fields, fewer hazardous substances emitted from computer equipment or from waste recycling, and ergonomic improvements. Agreements between TCO Development and the computer companies require companies to carry out active environmentally related work (in line with international standard ISO 14001 for environmental management). Because TCO requirements are taken into account in product development, the whole production process is affected.

Agreements have been reached with more than 100 companies, and this labelling system is now used for products including furniture and mobile phones. Project results have been positive for the users of labelled products and for workers at firms where the products are made. There are plans to expand labelling requirements to include a social dimension.

This project operates at no cost, as it is financed through the sale of licences to firms. Among other benefits, it has produced a workplace evaluation tool that can help trade unions and their members present their demands to management.

While the concept behind TCO labelling is solidarity, trade unions can also collaborate with others (e.g. people concerned about the environment, public authorities, and even manufacturers of IT equipment), raising issues and creating situations in which all parties benefit. The TCO label can be seen on over 200 million computer screens worldwide.

A Swedish Confederation representing 17 trade unions with a total of 1.2 million members can also represent all the world's computer users. This initiative has depended on a user perspective: all labeling requirements are for the user's benefit.

Swedish Confederation of Professional Employees (TCO)
(www.tco.se)

International Organization for Standardization – 14000 environmental management series
(www.iso14000-iso14001-environmental-management.com)

---

106 Based on the case study presented by Lars Bengtsson, representing the Swedish Confederation of Professional Employees (TCO), at the Nairobi Trade Union Assembly / WILL 2006.

Trade unions, despite differences in political power, member structure, internal organization and societal function, are clearly key actors in moving towards more sustainable production and consumption patterns. This is particularly true in that successful implementation of changes in the working environment depends, to a large extent, on the knowledge, support and acceptance of workers. Trade unions have a unique position and the power to facilitate changes in the working environment. They are involved in initiatives and policy-making processes at the local, regional, national and international levels. As a result of this multi-layered pattern of engagement, trade unions have a large number of organized workers, as well as expertise and communication channels. They have great potential to draw further participants and expertise into the process.

Moreover, members' traditional core interests (e.g. job creation, secure income levels and safe working conditions), which are still at the top of trade union agendas, are important issues that are also part of the sustainable consumption and production agenda. Job generation and corporate social and environmental responsibility are key issues in both developing and developed countries. These aspects can contribute not only to changing unsustainable consumption and production patterns, but also to generating new job opportunities, especially in poor countries.

In this context, the concept of sustainable consumption and production needs to be better understood. One mechanism for bringing this about could be to demonstrate benefits and best practices, as well as to more actively involve trade unions in the Marrakech Process.

Box 4.1.2

Other examples of trade union activities aimed at more sustainable consumption and production

- Flower Label Programme (FLP) – German Trade Union for Building Agriculture and Environment (IG-BAU), Germany (www.fian.de/fian/index.php?option=content&task=view&id=10&Itemid=50);

- Green Matters and Car Sharing Database – Prospect "union for professionals", United Kingdom (www.prospect.org.uk);

- Sustainable Agriculture – United Farm Workers of America (www.ufw.org);

- Plastic Bag Regulations – Congress of South African Trade Unions (COSATU) (www.anc.org.za) and National Council of Trade Unions (NACTU), South Africa (www. cosatu.org.za).

For further information, see (among numerous sources) Bernard Heins and others, The Role of Trade Unions in the Process towards Sustainable Consumption and Production, UNEP/Ecologic, 2004 (www.unep.fr/outreach/bi/labour.htm; or
www.ecologic.de/download/projekte/1850-1899/1883/1883_study.pdf).

The way ahead

Considering the importance and strategic position of trade unions, they need to be encouraged and supported in developing their own knowledge and theoretical concepts, as well as policies and programmes. Thus they can become full-fledged partners in moving towards sustainable consumption and production patterns. To this end, they could adopt a more integrated view of production patterns, including economic, environmental and social interests.

Trade unions could become more involved in identifying and analyzing the gains and losses experienced in different economic sectors during the transition process, while supporting workers from traditional industries in transferring more easily to new (and more sustainable) economic sectors. This would facilitate the shift towards more sustainable production and consumption patterns.

Some activities that could more actively engage trade unions in concrete initiatives towards sustainable consumption and production include (Heins and others 2004):

❑ Engaging trade unions more actively in concrete initiatives and projects at plant level. Trade unions could help to identify best practices for engaging with employers and workers in the promotion of sustainable consumption and production patterns;
❑ Encouraging partnerships and alliances with other stakeholder groups. Dissemination of best practices, e.g. through the UN Global Compact Learning Forum,[107] would help increase the number and effectiveness of alliances and co-operative efforts;
❑ Increasing trade unions' participation in sustainable development policy-making, specifically in the Marrakech Process. Given the existing infrastructure, networks and expertise, stronger participation in these processes by trade unions could significantly contribute to easing possible tensions between conflicting objectives.

Finally, there is a need for a more coherent and systematic approach to the study of trade unions' activities at the international, national and local level, one which could support an adequate assessment of their actual and potential contribution to the promotion of sustainable consumption and production.

References

- Heins, Bernard and others (2004). The Role of Labour Unions in the Process towards Sustainable Consumption and Production. Final Report to UNEP-DTIE. Ecologic for UNEP (www.unep.fr/outreach/bi/labour.htm; or www.ecologic.de/download/projekte/1850-1899/1883/1883_study.pdf June).

- UNEP (United Nations Environment Programme) (2002). Global Environment Outlook (GEO-3) (www.unep.org/geo/geo3).

- Worldwatch Institute (2004). State of the World 2004: Consumption By the Numbers (www.worldwatch.org/node/1783).

— (2005a). Global Fossil Fuel Consumption Surges. Press release, 8 May 2005 (www.worldwatch.org/node/1811).

— (2005b). Vital Signs (www.worldwatch.org/node/1057).

---

107 www.globalcompact.org.

4.2. Corporate social responsibility and accountability

*Cornis Lugt, Division of Technology, Industry and Economics, United Nations Environment Programme, **Gerd Albracht**, Occupational Safety and Health and Co-ordinator, Development of Inspection Systems, International Labour Organization, **Daniela Zampini**, Multinational Enterprises Programme, International Labour Organization, and **Corey Kaplan**, Development of Inspection Systems, SafeWork, International Labour Organization*

The Trade Union Assembly on Labour and the Environment / WILL 2006 included discussions on corporate social responsibility (CSR). Background material provided for this meeting used the term "enterprise social responsibility" (ESR), mindful of the fact that companies are of different sizes. In addition, not all companies are corporations and some companies are partially or fully state-owned.

In Nairobi, trade union representatives debated the meaning of CSR at length. Trade unions have had mixed feelings about CSR for many years, fearing that a general social agenda could divert attention from core labour issues. Moreover, in the last two decades international attention to sustainable development has challenged union leaders to consider the extent to which a traditional workers' rights agenda could open up and incorporate the broader issues faced by all societies.

In search of an acceptable definition of CSR

During the Trade Union Assembly, the discussions of the Working Group on Enterprise Social Responsibility and Accountability resulted in agreement on the core elements that participants felt should be part of any CSR definition, planning and action. The Working Group's suggestions and recommendations (Box 4.2.1) are an important reference for a future approach to CSR by the trade union movement.

Box 4.2.1

Recommendations of the Working Group on Enterprise Social Responsibility and Accountability,[108] Trade Union Assembly on Labour and the Environment / WILL 2006

Our Working Group asks this Assembly to call for:

1) **A greater commitment to education and training** – As CSR is a relatively new concept, we cannot assume that trade union leaders, members or managers understand it or know about its institutions, agreements and instruments. We therefore call on trade unions and central labour organizations to provide education and training in all aspects of ESR, in partnership with UNEP, the ILO, WHO, UNESCO, UNIDO and other agencies. Materials and other resources must be comprehensible, and where possible, education and training should jointly involve workers, trade unions and managers.

2) **Greater efforts to strengthen mandatory provisions for a level, appropriate playing field** – As effective ESR requires robust state action and control, we call on governments to provide the legislation and enforcement necessary to ensure that standards are observed by all enterprises.

---

108 The Working Group preferred the term "social responsibility" (SR) to the terms "enterprise social responsibility" or "corporate social responsibility" (see Recommendation 4).

Box 4.2.1 (...cont'd)

This means that the capacity of the state to protect workers, citizens and the natural environment must be increased in many countries, and that the line between enforceable and non-enforceable laws and instruments be clearly drawn.

3) **Action that differentiates bipartite and tripartite approaches from multi-stakeholder engagement** – Meaningful action for ESR requires the participation of workers and other affected parties. It is key to preventing corruption and reliable reporting. NGOs and other actors must be invited into the ESR process wherever possible; however, NGOs and multi-stakeholder consultation cannot be allowed to substitute for collective bargaining, good industrial relations, joint industry committees, or agreements that involve trade unions, employers and government. The unique capacity of trade unions to represent workers must be recognized.

4) **Finally, we call on all parties to "practise what they preach"** – Our group preferred the term "SR" (or "social responsibility"), because it implies that responsibility rests not only with companies, but also with governments, public sector organizations, trade unions and all other players. In accordance with this understanding:

We call on companies, whether large, small or medium-sized, to commit to implementation, accountability and reporting processes that are reliable, consistent and transparent. Sustainability reports must be more than PR exercises, but must be based on participatory monitoring and reporting that employs Global Reporting Initiative (GRI) guidelines.

We call on governments to ratify international instruments and to follow through with appropriate laws and enforcement practices, to directly promote tripartite and multi-stakeholder initiatives, and to require that social and environmental clauses be part of all public works and tendering processes. Governments that sign on to the OECD Guidelines for Multinational Enterprises must provide for strengthened "national contact points" and national networks for dialogue and implementation, as well as social observatories to monitor company behaviour.

We call on trade unions to take every opportunity to promote ESR; otherwise they fail in their responsibility to their members, societies and the environment. They must watch for violations of standards, and be prepared to make complaints to the ILO where serious violations of ILO instruments occur (as well to UNEP and other agencies and instruments as appropriate). Trade unions are called on to play a more active role to ensure socially responsible investment (e.g. pension funds, where they have the power to do so). We must do more to organize, monitor and publicize ESR cases (both positive and negative) and to provide active support to workers in countries where trade unions are too weak or oppressed to respond effectively to violations of ESR standards, or to basic principles such as those contained in the Global Compact.

In summary, the Working Group agreed that the following elements are fundamental:

❑ *The principle of "compliance plus voluntarism"* – voluntary approaches can only supplement mandatory aspects;
❑ *Integration* – all three pillars of sustainable development must be covered;
❑ *Consistency, transparency, accountability* – companies must account for social and environmental effects throughout the life-cycle of products, bridging environmental considerations and labour rights;
❑ *Multi-stakeholder engagement* – CSR action must include workers and trade unions, but it must also include meaningful participation and dialogue with NGOs, consumer associations and others;
❑ *The business case* – CSR is not charity, but an integral component of sound decision-making and business practice;

❑ *Democratic governance* – CSR must involve the engagement of workers in planning, documentation and strategy execution on an ongoing basis.

These important elements can guide trade union approaches to CSR in collective action and action at the company level. The issues addressed exist against a background of renewed CSR debate in recent years, driven by growing concern about the relationship of business to the rest of society. At the Davos World Economic Forum in 1999, UN Secretary-General Kofi Annan warned of a backlash against globalization and challenged business to promote core values in the global marketplace. He also called for "corporate citizenship", as is currently being promoted under the UN Global Compact (Box 4.2.2).

Box 4.2.2

The UN Global Compact's Ten Principles

The Global Compact is currently the world's largest CSR initiative, with over 3 000 participants and national networks in some 50 countries. Most of the participants are individual companies whose chief executives have signed up their commitment to the Compact's ten principles. Other participants include business associations, trade union bodies and international NGOs.

The Global Compact is a voluntary network. At its core are the Global Compact Office and six UN agencies.[109] Both UNEP and the ILO are actively involved in the Compact, acting as guardians of the environment and labour principles, respectively.

The Compact has two main objectives: to mainstream the ten principles in business activities around the world, and to catalyze actions in support of UN goals. To achieve these objectives, it offers facilitation and engagement through policy dialogues, learning, country/regional networks and projects.

The ten principles are:[110]

Human Rights
Principle 1: Businesses should support and respect the protection of internationally proclaimed human rights; and
Principle 2: Make sure that they are not complicit in human rights abuses.

Labour Standards
Principle 3: Businesses should uphold the freedom of association and the effective recognition of the right to collective bargaining;
Principle 4: The elimination of all forms of forced and compulsory labour;
Principle 5: The effective abolition of child labour; and
Principle 6: The elimination of discrimination in respect of employment and occupation.

Environment
Principle 7: Businesses should support a precautionary approach to environmental challenges;
Principle 8: Undertake initiatives to promote greater environmental responsibility; and
Principle 9: Encourage the development and diffusion of environmentally friendly technologies.

Anti-Corruption

Principle 10: Businesses should work against all forms of corruption, including extortion and bribery.

---

109 Office of the High Commissioner for Human Rights (OHCHR), UNEP, ILO, UN Development Programme (UNDP), UN Industrial Development Organization (UNIDO), United Nations Office on Drugs and Crime (UNODC).
110 The Global Compact's ten principles are derived from the Universal Declaration of Human Rights, the ILO Declaration on Fundamental Principles and Rights at Work, the Rio Declaration on Environment and Development and the UN Convention Against Corruption.

Perspectives and activities of UNEP and the ILO

In the *UN Global Compact Environment Principles Training Package* (UNEP 2005) corporate citizenship is defined as "a values-based way of conducting business in a manner that advances sustainable development, seeking positive impact between business operations and society, aware of the close interrelation between business and society as well as of companies, like citizens, having basic rights and duties wherever they operate." UNEP's work in this area has always underlined the importance of a business case approach,[111] and of following an integrated triple bottom line approach (i.e. one that covers economic, social and environmental issues).

From an ILO perspective, compliance with the law is the point of departure and CSR is the means by which enterprises give consideration to the impact of their operations on society and affirm their principles and values, both in their own internal methods and processes and in their interaction with other actors. CSR is a voluntary, enterprise-driven initiative and refers to activities that are considered to exceed compliance with the law. This view gives primacy to the role of law: both its implementation by governments, and the obligation of enterprises to comply with law.

In this respect, the ILO has often distinguished the current approach to CSR (which emphasizes its voluntary nature, multiple stakeholders and management of social impacts) from the social responsibilities of enterprises as defined in legally binding and non-binding instruments at the national and international levels – and as defined by society and the communities in which enterprises operate.

Issues normally addressed under the heading of CSR include business ethics, governance and accountability, codes of conduct, verification, certification, reporting, ethical investment, fair trade, partnership, regulation and voluntarism. To these issues, many of which relate to the *"how"* of implementing CSR, UNEP would add the *"goals"* of sustainable consumption, production and development. This recognizes that, as big companies grow, their environmental impact increases despite some resource efficiency gains. Many company codes of conduct are little more than general statements of business ethics. The question is how these codes and instruments can be used more effectively to benefit stakeholders, catalyze change within companies, raise awareness of interlinkages between production and consumption, and advance the concept of extended responsibility based on a life-cycle approach.

The ILO has found it helpful to review CSR-related initiatives, distinguishing between workplace initiatives (sometimes also referred to as "private standards"), accreditation and certification schemes, framework agreements, reporting initiatives, management frameworks and (inter)governmental initiatives.

Focusing on the areas of management and reporting, UNEP's work entails engaging business in industry sector initiatives, as well as in the Global Reporting Initiative (GRI), which is a cross-sectoral, multi-stakeholder initiative. UNEP's sector-based work includes initiatives with industries, such as the following:[112]

❑ Tourism (Tour Operators Initiative);[113]
❑ Finance (UNEP Finance Initiative);

---

111 "A business case is a structured proposal for business change that is justified in terms of costs and benefits." Excerpted from http://en.wikipedia.org/wiki/Business_case.
112 For the organizations mentioned in this chapter (with their websites), see the References at the end of the chapter.
113 The Tour Operators Initiative for Sustainable Tourism Development (www.toinitiative.org) was developed with the support of UNEP, UNESCO and the United Nations World Tourism Organization (UNWTO), which are full members of the Initiative.

- ❏ Information and communications technology (Global e-Sustainability Initiative);
- ❏ Advertising (Advertising and Communication Forum);
- ❏ Building and construction (Sustainable Buildings and Construction Initiative);
- ❏ Automobile manufacturing (Mobility Forum);
- ❏ Mining (the Cyanide Code).[114]

International calls, mandates and initiatives related to CSR

Questions about the role of business were echoed in debates at the World Summit on Sustainable Development (WSSD) in 2002, where the role of multi-stakeholder partnerships and the possibility of business being part of the solution received special attention. Among its outcomes, the Johannesburg Plan of Implementation (JPOI) called on private sector corporations to "enhance corporate environmental and social responsibility and accountability."[115]

In the following year, Decision 22/7 of the UNEP Governing Council mandated UNEP to further develop its work with business and industry in this field. One way this has been done is as part of the follow-up process to advance sustainable consumption and production (SCP), as addressed under Chapter III of the JPOI. UNEP's work in this field has been built on its earlier work related to Chapter 30 of Agenda 21 ("Strengthening the Role of Business and Industry")[116] and its activities to promote cleaner production, including the UNEP International Declaration on Cleaner Production (UNEP 1998). The Declaration on Cleaner Production has attracted many signatories from the private and public sectors in the developing world.[117]

The key point of reference for the ILO's work on CSR is its Tripartite Declaration of Principles concerning Multinational Enterprises and Social Policy (the MNE Declaration) (ILO 2001). The MNE Declaration is the only universal instrument on CSR that has been adopted by governments and by both employers' and workers' organizations. It sets out principles in the areas of general policies, employment, training, conditions of work, and industrial relations. To a large extent, these principles are equally applicable to both multinational and national enterprises.

To make the MNE Declaration an operational instrument and advance ILO's leadership in this area, the 295th session of the ILO Governing Body set strategic priorities for the 2005-07 InFocus Initiative (IFI) on Corporate Social Responsibility.[118] The IFI seeks to provide governments and

---

114 The International Cyanide Management Code for the Manufacture, Transport and Use of Cyanide in the Production of Gold (ICMI) is a voluntary industry programme for the gold mining industry to promote responsible management of cyanide used in gold mining; enhance the protection of human health; and reduce the potential for environmental impacts. To inform stakeholders of the status of cyanide management practices at certified operations, companies that become signatories to the Code must have their operations audited by an independent third party to demonstrate their compliance with the Code. Audit results are made public on www.cyanidecode.org.

115 "III. Changing unsustainable patterns of consumption and production" (paragraph 18) (www.un.org/esa/sustdev/documents/WSSD_POI_PD/English).

116 www.un.org/esa/sustdev/documents/agenda21/english/agenda21chapter30.htm.

117 The International Declaration on Cleaner Production is a voluntary but public statement of commitment to the strategy and practice of cleaner production. The Declaration was launched in October 1998 at Phoenix Park, South Korea, with 67 inaugural signatories. Signing ceremonies at other national and international venues have added Declaration partners to the Signatory List. The number of these regional and national signatories was over 1 700 at the time of writing. UNEP encourages government leaders, company presidents, NGO executive directors, business association presidents and other community leaders to publicly affirm their commitment and exercise leadership in cleaner production by signing and implementing the Declaration (www.uneptie.org/pc/cp/declaration).

118 www.oit.org/public/english/standards/relm/gb/docs/gb295/pdf/mne-2-1.pdf.

employers' and workers' organizations with new and valuable products that use the principles laid down in the MNE Declaration as the foundation of good CSR policy and practice.

At the international level, the ILO's MNE Declaration and the OECD Guidelines for Multinational Enterprises (OECD 2000) are the two key, governmentally endorsed sets of expectations that focus specifically on business's social responsibilities[119] The social and environmental responsibilities of business have also been addressed in more comprehensive intergovernmental agreements, notably Agenda 21 in 1992 and the Johannesburg Plan of Implementation (JPOI) in 2002.

Action by business and industry, including labour, received coverage in a whole chapter of the JPOI on SCP (Chapter III). Concerning corporate environmental and social responsibility and accountability, the JPOI asks for action to be taken to "encourage industry to improve social and environmental performance through voluntary initiatives, including environmental management systems, codes of conduct, certification and public reporting on environmental and social issues, taking into account such initiatives as the International Organization for Standardization (ISO) standards and Global Reporting Initiative guidelines on sustainability reporting."[120]

In 2000, two years before the WSSD, the UN had already been promoting CSR through the UN Global Compact. The Global Compact, launched at Davos in 1999, has formed part of an attempt to promote universal values and improve delivery and impact by working more closely with non-governmental partners, including trade unions, business and civil society organizations (Box 4.2.2).

The WSSD did not result in an international convention on corporate accountability, as some NGOs had hoped. Nevertheless, the years that followed have seen the start of a multi-stakeholder process to develop an international standard on social responsibility (SR). In 2004 the International Organization for Standardization (ISO) formally created a multi-stakeholder working group to begin developing what is to become a guidance instrument for social responsibility called ISO 26000.[121] In view of the widespread uptake of ISO management standards (e.g. ISO 14000 on environmental management and ISO 9000 on quality management) during the last ten years, the start of the ISO 26000 process has attracted much attention, as well as participation by national standards experts, business, labour, consumer organizations and NGOs. One impact of the process is recognition of the relevance of social dialogue and the input of social partners across a wide range of CSR issues. Many stakeholders have been involved, including UNEP, ILO, the Global Compact, the International Confederation of Free Trade Unions (ICFTU) and the International Organisation of Employers (IOE).

It is anticipated that the forthcoming ISO 26000 could serve as an instrument to foster greater awareness and wider observance of agreed sets of universal principles. The ISO governing bodies' resolution that began the process stipulated that the new instrument would not

---

119 The OECD Guidelines for Multinational Enterprises are recommendations addressed by governments to such enterprises operating in or from adhering countries. They provide voluntary principles and standards for responsible business conduct in a variety of areas, including employment and industrial relations, human rights, environment, information disclosure, combating bribery, consumer interests, science and technology, competition, and taxation (www.oecd.org/dataoecd/56/36/1922428.pdf).

120 www.un.org/esa/sustdev/documents/WSSD_POI_PD/English/POIChapter3.htm.

121 http://isotc.iso.org/livelink/livelink/fetch/2000/2122/830949/3934883/3935096/home.html?nodeid=4451259&vernum=

be a management system and would not be applicable to third-party certification. This is of basic importance, as it suggests that the concept of SR – which is the responsibility of all organizations, not just "corporates" – is too complex to be encapsulated in one simple, certifiable management system standard. It also serves to avoid a superficial standard that would undermine key international instruments focusing on specific areas such as environmental and labour standards. The process of formulating the ISO guidance on SR is expected to end in 2008.

Private voluntary initiatives and agreements

Businesses are encouraged to engage with trade unions and other stakeholders in a variety of voluntary private initiatives to promote CSR. Voluntary initiatives are non-legislatively required commitments or obligations agreed to by one or more organizations, often by companies making commitments to improve their environmental performance beyond legal requirements. These initiatives frequently take the form of negotiated agreements between industry and public authorities. Although voluntary, such an initiative may nevertheless be:

- ❏ Legally binding in the case of a signed, contractual agreement, and thus enforceable if broken;
- ❏ *Mandatory* if it becomes a condition for membership in an industry association;
- ❏ *Compulsory* if it becomes a de facto marketing requirement (e.g. in the case of ISO 14000 on environmental management) or when it has the same weight as traditional regulations, as in countries with an established consensus-based approach;
- ❏ *Used to encourage compliance* with existing laws.

At the international level, various industry associations, trade unions and NGOs have been involved in creating CSR-related international voluntary codes and guidelines. In the social field these include the Ethical Trading Initiative (ETI) or, in the context of the ILO, the Better Factories Cambodia initiative.

Not only has UNEP worked with partners in undertaking industry sector initiatives, as mentioned above, but it also took part in launching the Global Reporting Initiative (GRI) process in 1997 (Box 4.2.3).

Box 4.2.3

The Global Reporting Initiative (GRI)

The mission of the GRI is to develop and disseminate globally applicable Sustainability Reporting Guidelines for voluntary use by organizations in reporting on the economic, environmental and social dimensions of their activities, products and services. The initiative's goal is to raise corporate sustainability reporting to the level of rigour, credibility, comparability and verifiability of financial reporting. At a time when there is wide-ranging discussion of corporate governance, transparency and accountability, this goal is as relevant as ever.

The GRI process was launched in 1997 by the Coalition for Environmentally Responsible Economies (CERES) and UNEP. For UNEP, it is essential that corporate voluntary action be accompanied by verified sustainability reporting to display accountability and transparency.

The GRI has remained an ongoing, global, multi-stakeholder process of ongoing revisions and improvement of reporting guidelines. The new G3 version follows the earlier second version launched at WSSD in Johannesburg. Like its predecessor, the G3 version covers the core labour standards among its reporting indicators and provides disclosure items on, for example, corporate governance and management approaches to labour practices and decent work (GRI 2006).

Over the last ten years, leading corporations have increasingly adopted the GRI Guidelines. With its secretariat based in Amsterdam, the GRI operates with a multi-stakeholder Board (on which both business and labour are represented), a Stakeholder Council and a Technical Advisory Committee (TAC). The latter became operational in 2004, with experts in the fields of environment, labour, human rights, economics and finance, reporting and accounting. All of these governance bodies were closely involved in finalizing the third revision of the GRI Guidelines, leading up to the launch of the G3 GRI framework in October 2006.

There is consensus among all parties that CSR is not a replacement for the role of governments, and that it should not displace good governance. However, solutions to global challenges and the most pressing social problems are increasingly to be found at the intersection of regulatory and voluntary initiatives. A mix of public policy and private sector initiatives seems to represent the most effective strategy, whereby business addresses the needs of wider society while at the same time pursuing its own objectives. One example is provided by public-private partnership projects. For example, the ILO, in collaboration with Volkswagen and the German Technical Cooperation Agency (GTZ), is working to improve occupational safety and health among VW suppliers in Brazil, Mexico and South Africa.[122] Tripartite steering committees can play a key role in mainstreaming CSR through supply chains (Albracht 2006).

Challenges and areas for future cooperation

During WSSD, a labour conference on "Fashioning a New Deal" (Global Unions 2002) was jointly hosted by the ICFTU, the ILO, the Trade Union Advisory Committee (TUAC) to the OECD and UNEP (Global Unions 2002). At this conference it was agreed to start co-operative activities addressing workplace approaches to implementing labour, environmental and sustainable development objectives. The 2006 Nairobi Trade Union Assembly gave new impetus to follow up on this agreement. For example, ILO and UNEP are examining joint activities to promote CSR through supply chain management, taking as their point of departure the related work areas of environment, health and safety. A key aim will be to support investment by companies in human capital, engaging all employees to advance the values-based and triple bottom line business model introduced by CSR.

The Final Recommendation of the Trade Union Assembly on Labour and the Environment / WILL 2006 encouraged cooperation by UNEP, ILO and WHO in this field, including work in areas such as training and capacity building.[123]

Outsourcing and transnational supply chains have become a key feature of our globalizing world economy, raising new questions about standards applied in different parts of the world. Attempts to implement CSR via the supply chain have generally been made through a compliance-auditing system involving the adoption of codes of conduct by multinational enterprises (MNEs), requests that suppliers commit to such codes, and possible inspections of suppliers' workplaces by private means to verify that the commitments of both MNEs and suppliers are being met. Many codes of conduct refer to international labour standards and to universally agreed global business principles, such as those in the ILO Tripartite Declaration (ILO 2001). Some MNEs expect minimum environmental quality requirements from suppliers, including ISO 14001 certification. Codes of conduct can be categorized in terms of sectors, type (e.g. company codes, association codes, multi-stakeholder codes), scope (e.g. environmental, labour) and coverage (own operations, units, suppliers, etc.). As far as industry sectors are concerned, labour issues have tended to be concentrated in sectors such as garments, footwear, sporting equipment, toys and retailing. Environmental codes have more commonly been found in the chemicals, forestry, oil and mining sectors. These are process industries that have significant environmental impact and involve hazardous processes.

122 www.volkswagen-nachhaltigkeit.de/nhk/nhk_folder/en/leistungen/mitarbeiter/arbeit_und_gesundheit/ilo_zuliefererprojekt.html.
123 In article 4(a). See Chapter 4, section 3, "Education, capacity-building and knowledge sharing" by Lene Olsen, especially Box 4.3.4.

The challenge for ILO, UNEP, labour and business partners now is to examine how their related activities in this field can be linked to advance capacity building and more effective implementation (Box 4.2.4). For example, in South Africa the Ethical Trading Initiative contributed to the establishment of a local monitoring initiative called the Wine Industry Ethical Trade Association (WIETA), a multi-stakeholder coalition to improve labour practices in the wine industry of the Western Cape. Stakeholders include producers, retailers, trade unions, NGOs and the government.

The ILO is pioneering some research work to better understand the implication of the emerging partnership approach to the auditing of code compliance. Moreover, the biennial global benchmark survey of corporate sustainability reporting by UNEP and SustainAbility provides an ongoing opportunity to examine reporting on code appliance in the supply chain, referring to the relevant GRI reporting indicators (SustainAbility/UNEP 2004). The ILO's InFocus Initiative anticipates several activities, including developing knowledge on the different aspects of CSR, developing and providing training, and developing models of good practice.[124]

UNEP intends to build on its work related to greening the supply chain and sustainable procurement by public and private institutions. Under the Global e-Sustainablity Initiative, UNEP and ICT service providers and suppliers (with the support of the International Telecommunication Union) have been developing a suppliers' sustainability questionnaire for common use in their industry with the support of a shared, web-based data gathering system.[125] Improved usage of ICT in tracking and monitoring progress is one of a number of exciting areas where we can pool our experience and resources to promote corporate responsibility in favour of decent work and a clean, healthy environment for all.

---

124 www.oit.org/public/english/standards/relm/gb/docs/gb295/pdf/mne-2-1.pdf.
125 www.gesi.org.

Box 4.2.4

The Trade Unions Report Card: the CSR challenge for UN and labour organizations

UNEP Report Card: Trade Unions (Global Unions 2006) was prepared by the Trade Union Advisory Committee (TUAC) to the OECD and the International Confederation of Free Trade Unions (ICFTU) on the occasion of the 14th session of the UN Commission on Sustainable Development (CSD) in 2006. Among the conclusions presented in the Report Card are the following:

The undertaking by UNEP, ILO and WHO for new joint activities in the field of capacity building can follow up on the call in the JPOI, Chapter III on Consumption and Production, for "workplace-based partnerships and programmes, including training and education" [paragraph 17(d)]. Workplace assessments can be introduced at the shop floor level, between several plants, or for an entire region. Their checklist evaluations can lead to the adoption of programmes addressing concerns such as water and waste, energy efficiency, health and employment provisions. Training and education at the plant level on these issues can be targeted at both worker or employee representatives and operational managers. Moreover, they can be used to promote the inclusion and practical application of environment, chemicals and health related issues in agreements such as the Framework Agreements.[126]

---

126 For International Framework Agreements (IFAs), see Chapter 2, section 1, "Workers in the workplace and in their communities" by Lene Olsen, especially Box 2.1.3.

Box 4.2.4 (...cont'd)

From the above, it is clear that a major challenge awaits ILO, UNEP, the labour movement and other stakeholders in undertaking new joint activities to promote CSR.

This theme – part of the debate on globalization, competitiveness and sustainable development – has become increasingly important. For example, the European Commission plans to strengthen its co-operation with the ILO in order to promote decent work, including through a pilot project on trade and decent work indicators in developing countries. The implication of the CSR agenda for developing countries is a heavily debated topic. Some of these countries have focused on CSR as part of an integrated national competitiveness agenda. Indeed, initial findings confirm that competitiveness gains in a country may not be sustainable unless they are underpinned by responsible business practices

References

- Albracht, Gerd (2006). Enhancing OSH-Standards and Productivity through Supply Chain Management. Paper presented at the International Conference on Partnerships in Occupational Safety and Health Inspection: Strategies, methods and ideas for working in harmony across government and with industry to deliver integrated OSH inspection. Beijing, China, 13-14 April. (Oganized by the State Administration of Work Safety (SAWS), China, and the International Association of Labour Inspection (IALI) in co-operation with ILO.)

- GRI (Global Reporting Initiative) (2006). G3 Guidelines (released 5 October) (www.globalreporting.org/home; www.globalreporting.org/ReportingFramework/G3Online).

- Global Unions (2002). Fashioning a New Deal: Workers and Trade Unions at the World Summit for Sustainable Development (www.icftu.org/www/pdf/reportsouthafricaenglish.pdf).

— (2006). UNEP Report Card: Trade Unions. In Preparation for CSD-14 on Industrial Development, Energy, Climate Change and Air Pollution (www.global-unions.org/pdf/ohsewpQ_7a.EN.pdf).

- ILO (International Labour Organization) (2001). Tripartite Declaration of Principles concerning Multinational Enterprises and Social Policy (Third Edition) (www.ilo.org/public/english/employment/multi/download/english.pdf).

- OECD (Organisation for Economic Co-operation and Development) (2000). The OECD Guidelines for Multinational Enterprises. Revision 2000 (www.oecd.org/dataoecd/56/36/1922428.pdf).

- SustainAbility/UNEP (2004). Risk and Opportunity: Best Practice in Non-Financial Reporting. The Global Reporters 2004 Survey of Corporate Sustainability Reporting (www.uneptie.org/outreach/reporting/sustainability-reports.htm).

- UNEP (United Nations Environment Programme) (1998). International Declaration on Cleaner Production (www.uneptie.org/pc/cp/declaration).

— (2005). UN Global Compact Environment Principles Training Package (www.unep.fr/outreach/compact/trainpack.htm).

- (2006). Class of 2006. Industry Report Cards on Environment and Social Responsibility. Division of Technology, Industry and Economics (www.uneptie.org/Outreach/csd14).

4.3. Education, capacity-building and knowledge sharing

Lene Olsen, Bureau for Workers' Activities, International Labour Organization

Knowledge and education give people confidence, the feeling of personal achievement, and greater capacity to carry out their work and to adapt to changing technologies. Knowledge and education also help to prevent accidents. Knowledge is the basis for any meaningful action, and training and education are undoubtedly a major element in bringing about improvements. Almost all national, regional and international trade union movements have committed themselves to develop education programmes on their members' economic and social responsibilities. Knowledge is the cornerstone of trade union involvement in any issue, including environmental and sustainable development issues.

Numerous national and international meetings and conferences have highlighted the importance of education, capacity-building and knowledge sharing in relation to environmental and sustainable development issues. At the International Labour Conference in 1990, the International Labour Organization (ILO) adopted a Resolution on environment, development, employment and the role of the ILO. Clause 2(f) requests the Governing Body of the ILO to instruct the Director-General to "give increased attention to environmental education and training by integrating environmental considerations more effectively into training activities related to ILO programmes in all areas, including workers' and employers' education activities" (ILO 1990).

In the 1990s the ILO's Bureau for Workers' Activities (ILO/ACTRAV) carried out a project on Workers' Education and Environment. Under this project, numerous trade union organizations at various levels (mainly the workplace and national levels) and from different regions were involved in awareness raising and training activities and developed strategies and policies on environmental protection.

Today, trade unions need the capacity and qualifications to address issues which go beyond the workplace and even beyond the national level. For both trade union officials and the leaders of international companies, knowing and understanding the international context – and potential partners – is crucial when dealing with environmental policy and bargaining issues, or trying to influence international governance. Different forms of education are needed. International knowledge networks are growing, promoting changes in policy and practice and furthering environmentally sustainable development.[127]

From capacity-building to education

Although the ILO had undertaken a number of environmental training activities prior to 1990 (e.g. traditional vocational training, development of management approaches, workers' education, training programmes for employers' organizations), more focus was put on environmental activities in the 1990s.

Through ILO/ACTRAV's Workers' Education and Environment project, more than 60 workshops were held throughout Africa and Asia. Over 2 600 trade union members received training on the development of trade union policies and action plans in their

---

127 Also see Chapter 3, section 1 "Workers in the workplace and in their communities" by the same author.

workplaces and communities. A major focus was on how implementing ILO conventions could contribute to the sustainable development agenda. Dozens of case studies were developed showing how sustainable development issues had been integrated into trade union work on a practical level. Issues covered include occupational health and safety, transport of hazardous cargoes, water pollution control, and the impact of climate change on employment. Training materials were developed in English, French and Spanish. In addition, a number of local materials have been developed in several other languages, covering a variety of issues.

Trade union training and education, in the workplace and at national level, need to be adapted to local and national circumstances, taking into account language and cultural issues in particular. The level of knowledge, target groups, and issues to be addressed may change within and between workplaces, or within and between countries. A series of courses with the title "Trade Unions and the Environment", organized by the Trades Union Congress (TUC) of the United Kingdom, are an example of such a programme developed for workplace representatives (i.e. health and safety representatives and general shop stewards) interested in taking a wider view of their roles as environmental representatives (Box 4.3.1).

Box 4.3.1

United Kingdom: Courses on the environment for workplace representatives

The Trades Union Congress (TUC) of the UK has organized courses on "Trade Unions and the Environment" (TUC 2006a) to strengthen trade union responses to the climate change challenge by actively promoting sustainable policies at work. As part of this project, it has published **First Steps to a Greener Workplace** (TUC 2006b). In the summer of 2006 it also launched a "GreenWorkplaces" project aimed at building capacity to tackle energy and climate change issues at work.

Energy and other resources are consumed at workplaces, and waste is generated there. Workplaces are the most obvious starting point for tackling climate change and sustainable development issues. The TUC courses assist union representatives to:

- Develop a trade union approach to sustainable development;

- Share experiences of environmental issues at the workplace;

- Identify appropriate environmental legislation, policies and information;

- Engage union members in environmental issues at work;

- Develop an environmental action plan for the workplace.

Courses have been developed for unions across all sectors – including power generation, energy supply (coal, oil, gas), renewable energy, energy intensive sectors such as iron and steel and cement, and energy and resource intensive sectors ranging from the retail and office sectors to local government and the wider public sector.

Trades Union Congress (TUC) of the United Kingdom
www.tuc.org.uk

Different methods and techniques have been used in awareness raising activities and in the development of training and education courses for trade unionists on environmental issues. With the growing use of Internet, new technological tools have been added to the more traditional ones.

Common to any training and education activities is the question of access. While access to knowledge is key for workers, there are several preconditions. First, there is the matter of the very existence of courses, as well as the existence of knowledge by trainers and the possibility for workers to attend courses. Then there is the question of resources. Many unions in industrialized countries have the resources to develop courses on specific environmental issues, and to send union members to courses with paid educational leave, but unions in developing countries with limited resources do not always have these possibilities. North-South exchanges of both knowledge and financial resources are therefore very important. Also important is cooperation between employers and workers on education issues, especially concerning leave for education and paid educational leave.

Responding to global challenges

In addition to traditional forms of labour training, formal education courses have been developed to meet growing knowledge demands in terms of new issues, and to meet the challenges of globalization and cross-border concerns. The environmental agenda covers issues and problems which cannot be solved exclusively at the national level. Many environmental hazards are generated locally, but experienced globally.

An example of such a course is the one-year Master's programme on Labour Policies and Globalization offered in Germany by the University of Kassel and the Berlin School of Economics, in cooperation with the ILO, the international labour movement and academic partner institutions throughout the world (GLU 2006) (Box 4.3.2).

Box 4.3.2

Global Labour University

In 2002 the idea of a Global Labour University (GLU) was launched in order to facilitate discourse, stimulate research, and provide university-level qualification programmes on the political, economic and social dimensions of globalization for labour and trade union experts.

The immediate objectives of the GLU are to:

- Engage with trade unions and universities to develop and implement new university curricula to broaden the debate and knowledge base on labour and equity issues in universities;

- Qualify trade unionists and other interested labour experts, through internationally recognized university-based post graduate programmes, on the political, economic and social dimensions of globalization from a labour perspective;

- Establish a network for joint research on global labour issues;

- Facilitate discourse among trade unionists and researchers concerning the challenges of globalization.

The GLU network's first activity during its 2002-05 pilot phase was to develop and implement a pilot Master's course on Labour Policies and Globalization at the University of Kassel and the Berlin School of Economics in Germany. From 2007, the University of Witwatersrand (South Africa) will offer an additional Master's programme on Labour and Development within the GLU framework.

Cross-border training courses for trade unions are also carried out by the Workers' Activities (ACTRAV) Programme at the ILO's International Training Centre in Turin, Italy. The centre offers residential courses, field activities and distance learning. Among its strategic areas of training are international labour standards, employment policies and poverty reduction strategies, social protection and occupational safety and health, and social dialogue/collective bargaining and organizing.

Preconditions for access to courses at the international level are the same as at the national level, especially in terms of resources. In addition, the requirement to know a common language and (in the case of the one-year Master's course) the possibility to stay away from work for an entire year are not appropriate for everybody. However, in a multifaceted world, multifaceted solutions are required. The objective would be to find different solutions to different situations, and to different needs, when it comes to level of education, amount of time to be spent, financial resources and willingness to learn.

Knowledge networks

Knowledge networks among unions have existed for many years and have addressed different issues. With the use of Internet, such networks have increased in number and have been opened up to a broader group of members.

The Global Unions'[128] electronic forums are examples of how networks can use the Internet to reach out to (and co-ordinate) activities and campaigns. This method has also been used for activities related to environment. For example, it has facilitated information sharing by trade unions participating in meetings of the UN Commission on Sustainable Development (UNCSD), as well as making these unions' participation and work during UNCSD meetings more widely known.

An important part of trade union work within the framework of the UNCSD is the distribution of Country-by-Country Sustainable Development Profiles. These profiles include background information on all countries and on selected regions, industrial sectors and specific companies. They have become a guidepost for national and regional level actions on sustainable development issues. The profiles can be used by trade unions to plan national workplace action programmes. Other major groups may also use them as a basis for national decision-making and international analysis (Box 4.3.3).

---

128 "Global Unions" is a term used to indicate the major institutions of the international trade union movement.

Box 4.3.3

Country-by-Country Sustainable Development Profiles

Trade unions circulated the first version of these profiles to governments at the UN Commission of Sustainable Development (UNCSD) session in 2004. At the request of the EU Presidency, they consulted with other Agenda 21 major groups and then produced more complete versions. The profiles link economic, social and environmental data within a framework of sustainable development.

A new trade union Sustainable Development Unit was launched in July 2006 by the International Confederation of Free Trade Unions (ICFTU), the Global Unions Research Network (GURN), Sustainlabour and the Trade Union Advisory Committee (TUAC) to the OECD.

The Sustainable Development Unit's website makes country-by-country profiles available on a wide range of sustainable development issues, including:

- Energy;
- Climate change;
- Occupational health and safety;
- The 28 April International Commemoration Day (ICD) for Dead and Injured Workers;
- Asbestos
- HIV/AIDS;
- Trade union rights;
- Corporate accountability.

www.tradeunionsdunit.org/profiles

The Global Union Research Network (GURN), through a joint initiative with the International Confederation of Free Trade Unions (ICFTU), Sustainlabour and TUAC, has provided for even wider distribution of the profiles through its networks. Global Unions launched the GURN in cooperation with the ILO to ensure better information sharing, knowledge management, debate and joint research on global labour issues in order to promote sustainable livelihoods for working people and their families. Interlinkages between different trade union networks increase knowledge dissemination and broaden the awareness and involvement of workers.

Educating for the future

Education, capacity-building and knowledge sharing are important at all levels, from the workplace to the international level. The environmental agenda is international, and the issues it covers do not know any frontiers. That is why education, capacity-building and knowledge sharing are so important across borders – to learn from experiences elsewhere, to give new ideas to others, to set common priorities and goals, and to promote international rules and standards necessary for sustainable development. International education structures and knowledge sharing networks contribute to co-ordinated action and create synergies between activities. This enables the partners to become stronger in their multilateral actions.

It is therefore important to strengthen international cooperation in these fields, and to provide assistance to trade unions that do not have the capacity or financial resources to carry out their own educational programmes.

International organizations such as the ILO, WHO and UNEP should strengthen their cooperation on training to further build the capacity of workers regarding sustainable development issues (Box 4.3.4). The two organizations should combine their strengths – the ILO by using its tripartite structure (employers, workers and governments) and focusing on the international labour standards (i.e. the ILO Conventions and Recommendations) and UNEP through its expertise with respect to environmental issues.

Box 4.3.4

Areas for cooperation in capacity-building, training and the development of training materials

In article 4 (a) of the Final Resolution of the January 2006 Trade Union Assembly on Labour and the Environment (Annex III), the Assembly agreed on the importance of capacity-building and training, and the development of joint training materials for trade union leaders and workers, in the following areas (Trade Union Assembly on Labour and the Environment / WILL 2006):

- Climate change mitigation and adaptation: adaptation measures and their impacts on employment and workers' health;

- Sustainable consumption and production, including environmental management systems and occupational health and safety;

- Corporate environmental and social responsibility, as called for at the World Summit on Sustainable Development;

- Environmental content of global social dialogue, including framework agreements;

- Awareness and preparedness for emergencies at the local level including disaster management;

- Multilateral environmental agreements and law: improved awareness and understanding of their applicability to the workplace;

- Sound management of chemicals, including through evolving and newly adopted treaties or agreements, of industrial chemicals and of pesticides and enhancing the role of trade unions and workers in the implementation of the Strategic Approach to International Chemicals Management (SAICM), the European Union's REACH system and other programmes; and revitalizing the UNEP-ILO-WHO memorandum of understanding on the safe use of chemicals.

References

- International Labour Organization (ILO) (1990). Resolution concerning Environment, Development, Employment and the Role of the ILO. International Labour Conference, 77th Session (www.ilo.org/public/english/dialogue/actrav/enviro/backgrnd/resol3.htm).

— (1993). Workers' Education and the Environment (special issue of *Labour Education*, 93-1993/4).

- Trade Union Assembly on Labour and the Environment / WILL 2006 (2006). Final Resolution of the Trade Union Assembly at its First Meeting, Nairobi, January (www.unep.org/labour_environment/PDFs/TUALEfinalresolution-ENG.pdf).

- TUC (Trades Union Congress of the UK) (2006a). Trade Unions and the Environment: A TUC Education Short Course for Reps (www.tuc.org.uk/economy/tuc-12284-f0.cfm).

— (2006b). *First Steps to a Greener Workplace* (www.tuc.org.uk/economy/tuc-12460-f0.cfm).

4.4. The ITUC makes environment and sustainable development a priority

Lucien Royer, Trade Union Advisory Committee (TUAC) to the OECD, International Trade Union Confederation (ITUC)

The production of *Labour and the Environment: A Natural Synergy* coincides with the foundation Congress of the International Trade Union Confederation (ITUC), which took place on 1-3 November 2006.

At the foundation Congress, the International Confederation of Free Trade Unions (ICFTU), the World Labour Congress (WCL) and other independent trade unions merged into one new labour organization, the ITUC.[129] A new structural architecture was also agreed to by the European Trade Union Confederation (ETUC), the Global Union Federations (GUF) and the Trade Union Advisory Committee (TUAC) to the OECD.

This event will shape the future of trade union activities related to environmentally sustainable development. A "Workbook" produced for the Congress traces the recent history leading to this remarkable development. It also discusses various pathways for trade union actions in decades to come (ITUC 2006).

A call for trade unions to follow sustainable development pathways

At the United Nations, it required more than a decade for trade unions to obtain acceptance that social factors are intrinsic to sustainable development, along with environmental and economic factors. This acceptance took place at the 2002 World Summit on Sustainable Development (WSSD), bringing into focus a full range of issues considered important by workers everywhere: employment, income, livelihood, gender and poverty issues, along with participation policies that foster worker and trade union involvement in workplace and community decision-making. This development was an important precursor to any effective trade union focus on environmental protection, especially at the production and workplace levels – where occupational health and safety is of prime concern. Since the WSSD the world has received a mandate, at least at the policy level, to address social and environmental issues in a linked manner.

During the WSSD trade unions, the International Labour Organization (ILO) and the United Nations Environment Programme (UNEP) began to explore, as partners, how they can jointly work together to create a new understanding of sustainable development and integrate it with the practical implementation of solutions for workers and trade unions.[130]

In January 2006, nearly four years after the WSSD, the same partners (and others) came together in Nairobi to identify practical approaches at the Trade Union Assembly on Labour and the Environment / WILL 2006. Another "Workbook" became the Assembly's tool for crystallizing debate on such solutions, and for pointing the way for at least the next

---

129 See Chapter 2, section 2, "The trade union movement and environmental participation – shaping the change, renewing trade unionism" by Joaquín Nieto, especially Box 2.2.1.

130 For the WSSD and subsequent co-operative activities, see, in particular, the Introduction, Chapter 1 "Labour and the Environment: A Natural Synergy", Chapter 2, section 2 "Participating at all Levels" and Chapter 4, section 2, "Corporate social responsibility" by Cornis Lugt, Gerd Albract, Daniela Zampini and Corey Kaplan.

decade (Trade Union Assembly on Labour and the Environment 2006). The Workbook also provided some recent history related to its use, especially in facilitating discussions at two Assembly regional follow-up conferences for Latin America and Africa.[131]

The timing of the Assembly and of these follow-up conferences was particularly significant, as they took place just prior to the creation of the new ITUC and its adoption of a resolution addressing sustainable development issues. Together, these elements provide the nuts and bolts of a new trade union pathway for sustainable development, among other priorities. The collective wisdom of those attending the Assembly and its subsequent events, as reflected in the Workbook, was brought forward as input to the first resolution to be adopted by the ITUC – henceforth signalling a mandate for working in a concerted way on environment and sustainable development with its affiliates worldwide.

That this is a significant historical development has been recognized by many actors, most importantly ILO, WHO, UNEP and Sustainlabour. These bodies agreed to join union leaders at the first ITUC Congress in a special initiation event aimed at introducing a new sustainable pathway for workers and their organizations in years to come.

The ITUC Congress Workbook (ITUC 2006) was produced for a number of reasons. First, it sought to provide information about the evolution of thinking by trade unions on the implementation of sustainable development and environmental solutions. Second, it sought to provide a tool that could be used at national and sectoral levels to go beyond our current understanding and practice to bring about change through worker involvement at the workplace level.

The Workbook represents a crossroads for trade unions: it challenges workers to identify and address the world's environmental and sustainable development issues in their daily lives.

Integrating the environment into trade unions' sustainable development policy and action

The history of industrial development has led the world to a condition of environmental, social and economic crises, which has produced a number of inter-related problems and challenges for workers in areas. They include climate change, chemicals and hazardous substances, resource use and accessibility, and conditions of work, particularly as they relate to public health and occupational health and safety.

These workplace concerns are inextricably linked to issues faced by the public at large in all parts of the world. Current globalization trends have aggravated the situation with respect to poverty and the growing inequality of access to resources, services and health by large portions of the world population, especially the young and aged, women, the working poor, and those without employment or social protection to provide for their basic needs.

At the heart of current conditions is the basic fact that economic and production decisions continue to be made in isolation from the fundamental environmental and social dimensions of human life and health on our planet. Today meaningful decision-making has become the prerogative of the few, leaving most sectors of civil society disenfranchised or with dwindling influence and power.

---

131   The original version of this Workbook, updated to incorporate amendments made at the Trade Union Assembly / WILL 2006 and its outcomes, can be downloaded at www.unep.org/labour_environment/PDFs/WorkbookEN8.pdf.

At the workplace level and in the community, workers experience these crises along with everyone else. However, unionized workers have a greater margin of influence to bring about change, particularly when they negotiate with employers or co-operate with the UN system and other groups in civil society. Trade unions are in a position to inspire hope and enthusiasm for change.

A first priority for workers and trade unions is to change current patterns of production and consumption in an integrated manner, giving the highest priority to sustainable development approaches that link decision-making by the many to integrated social, environmental and economic outcomes. The collective challenge for each of us is to implement our vision of the future, country by country, sector by sector and workplace by workplace, while taking account of the different realities of different workers' lives. The integration and mutual reinforcement of the three pillars of sustainable development must remain a priority – this in the context of respecting cultural diversities, promoting democratic decision-making and seeking world peace.

Trade unions are being called upon to play a larger role in the struggle to save the planet. The focus of our engagement must continue to be the world's workplaces, which are at the core of production and consumption patterns. In addition, our strategies must focus on where problems are most serious (e.g. on issues related to climate change, chemicals and hazardous substances, resource use and accessibility, and conditions of work).

For change to take place, more co-operative industrial relations have to be developed among workers, trade unions and employers. Participatory processes must be strengthened and linked to the activities of governments and the constituencies they represent. Workplace participation must become a vehicle for employer accountability concerning a broad range of issues that relate to both occupational and community environments.

This will only occur if instruments and processes for social dialogue are developed. Resistance to changes whose purpose is to encourage sustainable development needs to be understood, especially as such changes impact the world of work. Awareness-raising, cooperation and mutual trust should become the trademark of joint decision-making, linking worker/union, employer and community efforts. Moreover, any programme should be linked to the promotion of *decent work*, providing jobs to deal with poverty but also to attain levels of socio-economic security. Moreover, *just employment transition* programmes are needed to maintain the livelihood of workers who lose their jobs or are displaced by change and require re-employment, compensation, re-training and education. Finally, our mission involves education, and it could not begin at a better time as this is the *International Decade of Education for Sustainable Development.*[132]

For these reasons, the relationship developed with UNEP must be linked to the decent work agenda of the International Labour Organization (ILO), and reflected in new relationships among the Environment, Health, Labour and Social Ministries of governments around the world. This agenda must also integrate public health links. ILO-UNEP-WHO involvement is crucial to linking occupational and community health and environment.[133] Global health challenges related to work encompass HIV/AIDS and asbestos exposure, among

---

132 http://portal.unesco.org/education/en/ev.php-URL_ID=27234&URL_DO=DO_TOPIC&URL_SECTION=201.html)
133 See the Final Resolution of the Trade Union Assembly/WILL 2006, article 4.

other issues. Damage to health in the working and living environments causes over 13 million deaths per year, almost six times the number of deaths from HIV/AIDS.[134]

Elements of a 1977 ILO-UNEP Memorandum of Understanding on environmental cooperation,[135] together with the joint ILO-UNEP-trade union activities initiated at the WSSD in 2002, provide a framework for stronger partnership building. These can serve as a model for other intergovernmental bodies developing strategies to address health, investment, trade and other key policy areas.

Governments must be urged to be more supportive of this new relationship in legislation, policy and action frameworks that involve civil society and Agenda 21 major groups. Governments must also affirm their responsibility and authority concerning proper governance of decision-making related to issues dealing with labour, environment and sustainable development. Public oversight, control and management must remain high government priorities, especially when dealing with access to information and technology transfer. Government roles in the provision of services must not be undermined or diminished, but strengthened through the deepening of democratic decision-making.

The trade union movement is committed to creating a transformation, extending from local to international levels that will challenge the limits of human development, thought and awareness and embrace the universal desire for a healthy planet, human emancipation and world peace.

References

- Sustainlabour (International Labour Foundation for Sustainable Development) (2004). Two Years Since Johannesburg: The Follow-up from a Labour Perspective (www.sustainlabour.org/documents/firstmeeting_report.pdf).

* Trade Union Assembly on Labour and the Environment / WILL 2006 (2006). The Workbook (Draft Version 8.0) (www.unep.org/labour_environment/PDFs/WorkbookEN8.pdf).

- ITUC (International Trade Union Confederation) (2006). Background Report for The Workbook. A trade union side event. Labour & Environment: Collective Commitments for sustainable development. "The Workbook". At The Founding Congress of the International Trade Union Confederation (ITUC) 1-3 November, 2006. Vienna, Austria (www.global-unions.org/pdf/ohsewpO_6h.EN.pdf).

- UNEP Division of Industry, Technology and Economics (UNEP DTIE) (2004) Managing the risks of chemicals. Special issue of Industry and environment, UNEP DTIE's quarterly review (www.uneptie.org; www.uneptie.org/media/review/ie_home.htm)

---

134 See, in particular, Chapter 3, section 3, "Occupational, environmental and public health" by Ivan D. Ivanov, Igor Fedetov and Monica Wehrle-MacDevette.
135 Memorandum of Understanding concerning cooperation between the International Labour Organization and the United Nations Environment Programme (www.ilo.org/public/english/bureau/leg/agreements/unep.htm).

Conclusion: Making the Environment a Focus of Collective Bargaining

During the last decade there has been a growing realization on the part of workers and trade unions that they need to focus on sustainable development issues.

There has also been an acknowledgement on the part of all the development partners that workers and trade unions have a key role to play in efforts to make companies, jobs and working conditions more environmentally/economically sustainable. Their knowledge and collective bargaining power are essential if the needed changes are to be made in time. Thus governments, businesses, civil society at large and labour are natural allies in the search for more sustainable development options.

With over 200 years of experience in protecting workers' rights, trade unions can make the environment a focus of collective bargaining, advocate more sensitive methods of using natural resources, and promote benefit-sharing and access to information and social and environmental justice. Environmentalists, in cooperation with workers, have a critical role to play in increasing awareness of environmental challenges and helping to build workers' capacity to implement relevant provisions of environmental conventions, legislation and policies.

One of the key messages of *Labour and the Environment: A Natural Synergy* concerns the need for action. The call is loud and clear: as a priority, the focus of all actors should be on acting – with respect to chemicals control and climate change, more sustainable production and consumption, and understanding (and planning for) global environmental changes. As pointed out by several authors, widespread changes in favour of "greener" technologies can create new job opportunities worldwide.

It is of crucial importance for everyone on the planet that all those concerned should do their best to understand and respond appropriately to environmental damage. This is strongly supported by the October 2006 report on climate change compiled for the government of the United Kingdom by Sir Nicholas Stern (former chief economist at the World Bank), which was published while this publication was being finalized.

One of the Stern report's main conclusions is that, in the 21st century, up to one-fifth of the world's wealth could disappear and the lives of billions be put at (greater) risk unless appropriate investments are made now in creating a global low-carbon economy. The report further emphasizes that the cost of investing in low-carbon technologies would be trivial compared with the potential damage that could be caused by climate change. Investing about 1 per cent of global GDP per year over the next 50 years could stabilize greenhouse gas concentrations at a level the report considers "high but acceptable".

If appropriate action is not taken, however, the Stern report warns of catastrophic disruptions to African economies in particular, owing to the effects of drought on food production. In addition, up to a billion people globally could lose their water supplies as glaciers disappear; hundreds of millions could be displaced by sea-level rises; and there could be more serious hurricane or tornado damage worldwide as storms become increasingly fierce. The cost of failing to act could approach US$4 trillion by 2100.

These conclusions further highlight some of the concerns raised by the authors of this publication. In Chapter 2, section 2, Joaquín Nieto reminds us that

> workers and trade unions are increasingly looking at the wider environmental implications of production and the need to promote a sustainable development agenda that goes beyond the workplace – an agenda covering, for instance, the effects of production on climate change. By increasing awareness among their members, trade unions increase citizen awareness and can contribute, in turn, to the modification of personal behaviour with respect to the environment. Workers and their trade unions not only want to be able to influence the way their company or organization affects their workplaces, lives, and surrounding communities and environment. They also want to influence how their employment is directly affected.

The newly adopted programme of the ITUC demonstrates that workers and trade unions have arrived in full force on the environment battlefield, as a driving force that should be counted on. Globalization is one of the most important issues for workers and trade unions in the 21st century. Despite the progress made by organized workers since the beginning of the Industrial Revolution, many workers today have few rights or have even lost rights that they once had. There are obvious connections between the struggle to make economies sustainable, and the struggle to make the benefits which workers in industrialized countries have fought for and won available to those everywhere. For example, pollution and climate change are problems that can only be attacked successfully at the international level. Environmental conditions, and likewise working conditions, in any part of the world affect us all. Again, in regard to just transition, people globally need decent jobs and a "decent" environment.

The way forward

The way forward lies in understanding the mutually supportive concepts of environmental and economic sustainability. Environmental sustainability means economic sustainability. Workers and trade unions need to support and contribute to the necessary shift in post-modern industrialization and its models. They have long been concerned with balancing economic and social benefits. Today these benefits have to be considered in the context of (mitigatable) health and environmental risks.

The commitment of UNEP, ILO and WHO to collaborate with trade unions in advancing the environmental agenda will provide an opportunity to fully extend this agenda to the world of labour. Avenues for these international organizations (and others) to explore, in cooperation with workers and trade unions, will primarily focus on the theme of labour and the environment and how it should be linked with the ongoing debate concerning globalization and the environment.

Based on discussions during the Trade Union Assembly on Labour and the Environment / WILL 2006, and on the papers subsequently collected in *Labour and the Environment: A Natural Synergy*, there is clearly widespread agreement that the establishment of a conceptual framework for Labour and the Environment, so as to continue exploring the nexus between the two (e.g. through case studies and learning-by-doing experiences), should be pursued. This could include replication/adaptation of successful initiatives reported in the case studies presented during the Assembly and in this publication.

The ultimate goal is to meet the collective challenge of preserving the world for future generations, including through drawing on the heritage of worker and trade union activities in order to promote sustainable development. Without any doubt, the future lies in finding innovative ways to deliver ecosystem services that satisfy the needs of human beings. While credit should be given for the successes (and even the good intentions) of the past, it is now urgent for governments, international organizations, business and industry, and civil society – in cooperation with labour and trade unions – to act!

Annex 1 - Final Resolution of the Trade Union Assembly on Labour and the Environment / WILL 2006, at its First Meeting

1. The Assembly *agreed* on the following objectives:

    (a) To strengthen the link between poverty reduction, environmental protection and decent work. Decent and secure jobs are essential for people to have a sustainable livelihood. Creating decent and secure jobs is only possible, however, if environmental sustainability is attained: hence the need to embrace the poverty reduction and sustainable development goals contained in the Millennium Declaration and Johannesburg Plan of Implementation through the promotion of decent employment and environmental responsibility. This must also include the mainstreaming of gender issues;

    (b) To integrate the environmental and social dimensions of sustainable development with a rights-based approach. Fundamental rights of workers such as freedom of association and collective bargaining must be respected if workers and their unions are to be able to engage in strategies for sustainable development. Moreover, human rights must include the universal, equitable, egalitarian and environmentally sound access to basic resources such as water and energy;

    (c) To establish effective and democratic governance to ensure sustainable development and, to that end, to reinforce the role of national public authorities, to establish the rules necessary to govern global markets and firms and to ensure both the compliance of business with law and regulations and also their wider accountability and responsibility, with a view to achieving the goals of sustainable development;

    (d) To take urgent action on climate change in support of the United Nations Framework Convention on Climate Change and its Kyoto Protocol; to develop new and additional agreements for both developed and developing countries, taking account of common but differentiated responsibilities; to anticipate and minimize the negative effects and maximize the positive effects on employment of mitigation; and to ensure the participation of trade unions in decision-making on climate change strategies;

    (e) To implement the Johannesburg goals on chemicals to make industry prove that chemicals used are safe for workers, consumers, communities and the environment; in the context of the Stockholm Convention on Persistent Organic Pollutants, to ensure the substitution of the most dangerous substances; and to ensure concerted global action through the adoption of the Strategic Approach to International Chemicals Management (SAICM) and its follow-up, and, in addition, to promote the finalization and implementation of the European Union's regulatory framework for the registration, evaluation and authorization of chemicals, to be known as the REACH system;

    (f) To promote sustainable production and consumption patterns through the reinforcement of cleaner production centres and the dissemination and transfer of technology;

(g) To introduce policies for just employment transition as a central feature of environmental protection and to ensure that workers negatively affected by changes are provided with safe and decent employment alternatives;

(h) To enhance the dialogue between labour and management, consultation and negotiation in the workplace on sustainable development, and social dialogue at the sectoral, national and international levels in both public and private sectors, to use appropriate tools to increase social and environmental responsibility and accountability of enterprises through both trade union and multi-stakeholder participation in genuine initiatives and to ensure that corporate social responsibility involves both compliance with law and voluntary initiatives;

(i) To enhance cooperation and coherence between international rules and conventions on environment and sustainable development. This is to be achieved through strengthened cooperation between the United Nations Environment Programme, the International Labour Organization, the World Health Organization and related environment, social, labour and health ministries;

(j) To link occupational health to environmental and public health policy and practice; while raising standards of occupational health and safety as an objective in its own right, to reinforce the International Labour Organization conventions and programmes to develop and promote it; to take account of the need for differentiated approaches between developed and developing countries; to use this as a central element of campaigns to fight HIV/AIDS; to prevent worker death, injury and illness from the effects of chemicals or dangerous substances, such as asbestos; and to ensure the right to reproductive health for women and men;

2. To achieve these objectives, the trade union representatives at the Assembly commit themselves to strengthening trade union action on sustainable development and to working:

(a) For the reform of government policies and practice, in particular by facilitating the transition to sustainable production and consumption in workplaces and the introduction of workers' environmental rights and participation;

(b) For the ratification and implementation of key conventions and instruments covering both the environment and the relevant International Labour Organization conventions, while promoting employment and social policies to make decent employment a key part of environmental protection, sustainable development and poverty eradication;

(c) For the development of capacity-building and training programmes to advance integration of the social economic and environmental pillars of sustainable development, including integrated implementation of the principles of the United Nations Global Compact, recognizing the particular importance of the protection of women;

(d) For the assessment, planning, implementation and monitoring of initiatives for environmentally safe and sustainable production and consumption, and also for the transfer of clean technology and development of technology assessment at the sectoral level;

(e) For the more effective application of tools to promote the social and environmental responsibilities of business, including agreed public instruments such as the

OECD Guidelines for Multinational Enterprises, the ILO Tripartite Declaration of Principles Concerning Multinational Enterprises and Social Policy, as well as, where appropriate, private initiatives such as sustainability reporting through the Global Reporting Initiative, and, where such systems exist, the use of workers' capital in pension funds;

(f) For the application at the global level of proposals contained in the European Union REACH programme on chemicals to regulate, within the context of the precautionary principle, the responsibility and liability of producers to trace and detect dangerous chemical substances;

(g) For the negotiation of global framework agreements with companies that incorporate environmental and sustainable development commitments and, where relevant, for the strengthening of the information rights of works councils;

(h) For the monitoring of Governments' investment and procurement practices and regulation, privatization and land-use policies, so as both to integrate social and environmental objectives and to ensure human rights and equity with respect to access to resources such as water and energy;

(i) For endeavours, mounted together with civil society allies, to encourage workplace and community action and awareness-raising among the members of trade unions, for example, through dialogue with community stakeholders and with the involvement of Agenda 21 major groups in decision-making;

(j) For effective prevention and responses to natural and industrial disasters with appropriate environmental legal responsibility;

(k) For a complete global ban on asbestos use, for its safe handling and disposal in accordance with the decisions of the Parties to the Basel Convention on the Control of Transboundary Movements of Hazardous Wastes and Their Disposal and for its inclusion in the Rotterdam Convention on the Prior Informed Consent Procedure for Certain Hazardous Chemicals and Pesticides in International Trade, and also for the promotion of integrated and workplace-based approaches to fighting HIV/AIDS.

3. The trade union representatives at the Assembly further commit themselves to working for increased trade union awareness at all levels on these issues in their own organizations worldwide, with a view to the adoption of policy and implementation plans for local, national and international action on the outcomes of this Assembly and to integrate this work at the sectoral level. They recommend that this global assembly is followed up regionally in Latin America, Africa and Asia.

4. The trade union representatives welcome the common platform between the United Nations Environment Programme, the International Labour Organization and the World Health Organization. The three organizations will explore the following opportunities for further action, as a follow-up to the Trade Union Assembly on Labour and the Environment:

(a) To undertake capacity-building and training, and the development of joint training materials for trade union leaders and workers in the following areas:
   • Climate change mitigation and adaptation: adaptation measures and their impacts on employment and workers' health;
   • Sustainable consumption and production, including environmental management systems and occupational health and safety;

- Corporate environmental and social responsibility, as called for at the World Summit on Sustainable Development;
- Environmental content of global social dialogue, including framework agreements;
- Awareness and preparedness for emergencies at the local level including disaster management;
- Multilateral environmental agreements and law: improved awareness and understanding of their applicability to the workplace;
- Sound management of chemicals, including through evolving and newly adopted treaties or agreements, of industrial chemicals and of pesticides and enhancing the role of trade unions and workers in the implementation of the Strategic Approach to International Chemicals Management (SAICM), the European Union's REACH system and other programmes; and revitalizing the UNEP-ILO-WHO memorandum of understanding on the safe use of chemicals;

(b) To facilitate the engagement of the labour movement with public authorities, for example, in public services delivery;

(c) To replicate the successful case studies presented at the Assembly and, to that end, to create and maintain a website to collect the case studies and to consider their possible publication;

(d) To promote the engagement of trade unions with other major groups, including multi-stakeholder dialogue to address the sustainable development agenda;

(e) To undertake a study on the incorporation of just employment into environmental policy design;

(f) To promote environmentally and socially responsible job growth;

(g) Jointly to review implementation of agreements on a regular basis;

(h) To provide a model for joint, integrated planning among the different sectors, such as the Health and Environment Linkages Initiative (HELI) of the World Health Organization and the United Nations Environment Programme;

(i) To invite the World Health Organization to present a global action plan on occupational health to the World Health Assembly in 2007, with contributions from the International Labour Organization and the United Nations Environment Programme;

(j) To provide an analysis of the health aspects of the transition to sustainable production, including the health consequences of changes in the employment situation.

Abbreviations

ACGIH	American Conference of Governmental Industrial Hygienists (USA)
ACTRAV	Bureau for Workers' Activities (ILO)
AFL-CIO	American Federation of Labor and Congress of Industrial Organizations (USA)
AGOA	African Growth and Opportunity Act
CAW	Canadian Auto Workers Union
CCOO	*Confederación Sindical de Comisiones Obreras* (Spain)
CDM	Clean Development Mechanism (Kyoto flexible mechanism)
CERs	Certified emission reductions
CFDT	*Confédération Française Démocratique du Travail* (France)
CGT	*Confederación General de Trabajo* (Argentina)
CGT-FO	*Confédération Générale du Travail-Force Ouvrière* (France)
CITUB	Confederation of Independent Trade Unions of Bulgaria
COSATU	Congress of South African Trade Unions
CSR	Corporate social responsibility
CTRN	*Central de Trabajadores Rerum Novarum* (Costa Rica)
DGB	*Deutscher Gewerkschaftsbund*
EIA	Energy Information Administration (USA)
EPR	Extended Producer Responsibility
ESR	Enterprise social responsibility
ETI	Ethical Trading Initiative
ETUC	European Trade Union Confederation
FGTB	Federation of Belgian Workers
FIDD	*Fonds d'investissement en développement durable* (Québec, Canada)
FNPR	Federation of Independent Trade Unions of Russia
GDP	Gross domestic product
GEO	Global Environment Outlook
GHS	Globally Harmonized System of Classification and Labeling of Chemicals
GLU	Global Labour University
GNP	Gross national product
GRI	Global Reporting Initiative
GUF	Global Union Federation
GURN	Global Union Research Network
HELI	Health and Environment Linkages Initiative (UNEP/WHO)
IARC	International Agency for Research on Cancer (WHO)
ICCM	International Conference on Chemicals Management
ICD	International Commemoration Day for Dead and Injured Workers

ICEM	International Federation of Chemical, Energy, Mine and General Workers' Unions.
ICFTU	International Confederation of Free Trade Unions
ICSC	International Chemical Safety Card
ICT	Information and communications technology
IEA	International Energy Agency
IFA	International Framework Agreement
IG-BAU	German Trade Union for Building, Agriculture and Environment
ILO	International Labour Organization
IMEC	International Maritime Employers' Committee
IMF	International Monetary Fund
IOE	International Organization of Employers
IPCC	Intergovernmental Panel on Climate Change
ITF	International Transport Workers' Federation
ITGLWF	International Textile, Garment and Leather Workers Federation
ITUC	International Trade Union Confederation
IUF	International Union of Food, Agricultural, Hotel, Restaurant, Catering, Tobacco and Allied Workers' Associations (IUF)
JI	Joint Implementation (Kyoto flexible mechanism)
JPOI	Johannesburg Plan of Implementation
LO Norway	Norwegian Confederation of Trade Unions
MA	Millennium Ecosystem Assessment
MDG	Millennium Development Goal(s)
Mercosur	*Mercado Común del Sur* (Southern Common Market)
NACTU	National Council of Trade Unions (South Africa)
NAFAU	Namibian Food and Allied Workers' Union
NEPAD	New Partnership for Africa's Development
NLC	Nigeria Labour Congress
NOAA	National Oceanic and Atmospheric Administration (USA)
OECD	Organisation for Economic Cooperation and Development
OHSE	Occupational health, safety and environment
OHSEI	Asian Workers Occupational Health, Safety and Environment Institute
PROSPECT	Trade union (UK)
PSI	Public Services International
REACH	Registration, Evaluation and Authorization of Chemicals
REN21	Renewable Energy Policy Network
SAICM	Strategic Approach to International Chemicals Management
SCP	Sustainable Consumption and Production
TCO	Swedish Confederation of Professional Employees

TUAC	Trade Union Advisory Committee to the OECD
TUC	Trades Union Conference of the United Kingdom
UFW	United Farm Workers of America
UNCED	UN Conference on Environment and Development
UNCSD	UN Commission on Sustainable Development
UNEP	United Nations Environment Programme
UNEP DTIE	UNEP Division of Technology, Industry and Economics
UNEP FI	UNEP Financial Initiative
UNIDO	UN Industrial Development Organization
WAVE	Women as the Voice for the Environment
WBCSD	World Business Council for Sustainable Development
WCL	World Conference of Labour
WEN	Women's Environmental Network
WHO	World Health Organization
WILL	Workers' Initiative for a Living Legacy
WMO	World Meteorological Organization
WRI	World Resources Institute
WSSD	World Summit on Sustainable Development

Glossary

- Adaptation: In biology an adaptation may be an evolving anatomical structure, physiological process or behavioural trait. This term is also used to refer to ways to live with, or benefit from, climate change (particularly global warming).

- Certified emission reductions (CERs): Units for measuring carbon credits. Each CER is equivalent to one tonne of CO_2 emission reduction. See clean development mechanism, Joint Implementation, Kyoto flexible mechanisms.

- Clean development mechanism (CDM): Under the clean development mechanism, Annex I Parties to the Kyoto Protocol may implement projects in non-Annex I Parties that reduce emissions, and use the resulting certified emission reductions (CERs) to help meet their own Kyoto emission targets. The CDM also aims to help non-Annex I Parties achieve sustainable development, and to contribute to the ultimate objective of the UN Framework Convention on Climate Change (UNFCCC) (http://unfccc.int/kyoto_protocol/mechanisms). See certified emission reductions (CERs), Joint Implementation, Kyoto flexible mechanisms.

- Collective agreement: Labour contract between an employer and one or more trade unions. See collective bargaining.

- Collective bargaining: Process of negotiation between trade union representatives and employers (or employers' organizations) on the terms and conditions of employment, e.g. wages, hours of work, working conditions and grievance procedures, as well as trade union rights and responsibilities. The results of such negotiations are sometimes referred to as a collective bargaining agreement (CBA) or a collective employment agreement (CEA).

- Corporate citizenship: Values-based manner of conducting business so that it promotes good citizenship, e.g. by working towards sustainable development. Corporate citizenship seeks to ensure that the impacts of business operations on society are positive, and that companies are aware of the close inter-relations between the two, as well as of the basic rights and responsibilities of companies and citizens wherever the companies operate.

- Corporate social responsibility (CSR)/enterprise social responsibility (ESR): "The Trade Union Assembly on Labour and the Environment included discussions of corporate social responsibility (CSR). Background material provided for this meeting used the term 'enterprise social responsibility' (ESR), mindful of the fact that companies are of different sizes. Not all of them are corporations. In addition, some are partially or fully State-owned. Trade union representatives debated the meaning of CSR at length. For many years trade unions have had mixed feelings about CSR, fearing that a general social agenda could divert attention from core labour issues. Moreover, in the last two decades international attention to sustainable development has challenged union leaders to consider the extent to which a traditional worker rights agenda can open up and incorporate the broader issues faced by all societies." From Chapter 4, section 2, "Corporate social accountability and responsibility" by Cornis Lugt, Gerd Albracht, Daniela Zampini and Corey Kaplan.

- Decent work: "Sums up the aspirations of people in their working lives. It involves opportunities for work that is productive and delivers a fair income, security in the workplace and social protection for families, better prospects for personal development and social integration, freedom for people to express their concerns, organize and participate in the decisions that affect their lives and equality of opportunity and treatment for all women and men." Definition from the International Labour Organization (ILO) web page "Decent work – the heart of social progress" (www.ilo. org/public/english/decent.htm). See working poor.

- Ecological goods and services: "The benefits arising from the ecological functions of healthy ecosystems. Such benefits accrue to all living organisms, including animals and plants, rather than to humans alone. However, there is a growing recognition of the importance to society that ecological goods and services provide for health, social, cultural, and economic needs. Examples of ecological goods include clean air, and abundant fresh water. Examples of ecological services include purification of air and water, maintenance of biodiversity, decomposition of wastes, soil and vegetation generation and renewal, pollination of crops and natural vegetation, groundwater recharge through wetlands, seed dispersal, greenhouse gas mitigation, and aesthetically pleasing landscapes. The products and processes of ecological goods and services are complex and occur over long periods of time." From http://en.wikipedia. org/wiki/Ecological_goods_and_services.

- Energy certificates: Tradable renewable energy certificates represent "the certified generation of one unit of renewable energy (typically one MWh). These certificates allow trading or renewable energy obligations among consumers and/or producers, and in some markets like the United States allow anyone to purchase separately the green power 'attributes' of renewable energy." Utility green pricing occurs when "a utility offers its customers a choice of power products, usually at differing prices, offering varying degrees of renewable energy content. The utility guarantees to generate or purchase enough renewable energy to meet the needs of all green power customers." Definitions from the REN21 Renewable Energy Policy Network (www. ren21.net). The United States Department of Energy's "Energy and Energy Efficiency" web page provides this definition of certificates: "Renewable energy certificates (RECs), also known as green certificates, green tags, or tradable renewable certificates, represent the environmental attributes of the power produced from renewable energy projects and are sold separately from commodity electricity. Customers can buy green certificates whether or not they have access to green power through their local utility or a competitive electricity marketer. And they can purchase green certificates without having to switch electricity suppliers" www.eere.energy.gov/greenpower/markets/ certificates.shtml?page=0).

- Environmental health: "Comprises those aspects of human health, including quality of life, that are determined by physical, chemical, biological, social, and psychosocial factors in the environment. It also refers to the theory and practice of assessing, correcting, controlling, and preventing those factors in the environment that can potentially affect adversely the health of present and future generations." Definition from the World Health Organization (WHO) Public Health and Environment (PHE) web page (www.who.int/phe/en/).

- Extended Producer Responsibility (EPR): "Strategy designed to promote the integration of environmental costs associated with products throughout their life cycles into the market price of the products." Definition from Extended Producer Responsibility: A Guidance Manual for Governments, OECD, 2001.

- Fair trade: The mission of Fairtrade Labelling Organizations International (FLO), one of the world's largest fair trade standard-setting and certification bodies, is to "esnable sustainable development and empowerment of disadvantaged producers and workers in developing countries" (www.fairtrade.net/support_fairtrade.html). Labelled fair trade goods range from crafts to agricultural commodities (e.g. coffee). As a social movement, fair trade focuses on exports from developing to industrialized countries and on aid to producers in the former.

- Genetic resources/material: Genetic resources are material of actual or potential value; genetic material means any material of plant, animal, microbial or other origin containing functional units of heredity. (Definition from the 1992 UN Convention on Biological Diversity). One of this Convention's three objectives, as set out in its Article 1, is the "fair and equitable sharing of the benefits arising out of the utilization of genetic resources, including by appropriate access to genetic resources and by appropriate transfer of relevant technologies, taking into account all rights over those resources and to technologies, and by appropriate funding."

- Global Union Federations (GUFs): International federations of national and regional trade unions, which are organized in specific public and private occupational sectors. Most of the world's major trade unions belong to one or more GUFs.

- Green agreement/clause: Any type of agreement or clause whose purpose is to promote environmental protection or sustainability. "Numerous collective agreements, including 'green' clauses, have … been signed, as have specific 'green agreements' at the local and national level. The aim of all these agreements is to set out commitments on environmental issues, identify each partner's responsibilities under the agreements, identify procedures, and create a structure for working on common priorities and a policy on environmental issues. At the workplace level environmental issues can include purchasing and recycling policies aimed at environmental protection. Such policies favour, among other things, low-energy lighting, low fuel-consuming vehicles, biodegradable cleaning materials, wood from environmentally well-managed forests, recycled paper and elimination of excessive packaging." From Chapter 2, section 1, "Workers in the workplace and in their communities" by Lene Olsen.

- Green chemistry: "Innovative chemical technologies that reduce or eliminate the use or generation of hazardous substances in the design, manufacture, and use of chemical products." Definition from the United States Environmental Protection Agency (US EPA) Green Chemistry Mission home page (www.epa.gov/greenchemistry).

- Green power purchasing/green marketing: "Voluntary purchases of green power by residential, commercial, government, or industrial customers, from utility companies, from a third-party renewable energy generator (also called 'green marketing'), or with 'renewable energy certificates'." Definition from The Renewables 2005 Global Status Report (www.ren21.com).

- Joint Implementation (JI): The basic principles of the Joint Implementation (JI) mechanism are defined in Article 6 of the Kyoto Protocol: "For the purpose of meeting its commitments … any Party included in Annex I may transfer to, or acquire from, any other such Party emission reduction units resulting from projects aimed at reducing anthropogenic emissions by sources or enhancing anthropogenic removals by sinks of greenhouse gases in any sector of the economy" provided that certain (participation) requirements are fulfilled. Under JI, an Annex I Party (with a commitment inscribed in the Protocol's Annex B) may implement an emission reduction project or a project that enhances removals by sinks in the territory of another Annex I Party (with a commitment inscribed in Annex B of the Protocol) and count the resulting emission reduction units (ERUs) towards meeting its own Kyoto target (http://unfccc.int/kyoto_protocol/mechanisms). See certified emission reductions (CERs), clean development mechanism (CDM), Kyoto flexible mechanisms.

- Just transition: Process that predicts or assesses the social security and employment impacts of change on workers and communities due to social, economic and environmental factors, and then institutes a transition process to address these impacts. "There is no single Just Transition programme. Any specific solutions must be adaptable enough to accommodate a wide variety of needs. There will be different types of transition programmes according to circumstances, and the issues at stake." From the Canadian Communications, Energy and Paperworkers Union website (www.cep.ca/.policies).

- Kyoto flexible mechanisms: The Clean Development Mechanism (CDM) and Joint Implementation (JI) are the Kyoto Protocol's two project-based mechanisms that may be used by Annex I Parties to fulfil their Kyoto emission reduction targets. See certified emission reductions (CERs), clean development mechanism (CDM), Joint Implementation (JI).

- Marrakech process: Process to promote concrete project implementation and progress on the ten-year UNEP Sustainable Consumption and Production (SCP) framework of programmes. It includes regular global and regional meetings, supported by informal expert task forces and roundtables.

- Mitigation: Activity whose purpose is to prevent or reduce damage (e.g. an environmental mitigation measure).

- Renewables: Natural resources (e.g. forests) or energy sources (e.g. the sun, wind, waves) which can be replaced or can replenish themselves.

- Social shield/social protection: "Social protection refers to a set of benefits available (or not available) from the state, market, civil society and households, or through a combination of these agencies, to the individual/households to reduce multi-dimensional deprivation. This multi-dimensional deprivation could be affecting less active poor persons (e.g. the elderly, disabled) and active poor persons (e.g. unemployed). This broad framework makes this concept more acceptable in developing countries than the concept of social security. Social security is more applicable in the conditions, where a large number of citizens depend on the formal economy for their livelihood. Through a defined contribution, this social security may be managed. But, in the context of a widespread informal economy, formal social security arrangements are almost absent for the vast majority of the working population. Besides, in developing countries, the state's capacity to reach the vast majority of the poor people may be limited because of its limited resources. In such a context, multiple agencies that could provide for social protection are important for policy consideration. The framework of social protection is thus capable of holding the state responsible to provide for the poorest sections by regulating non-state agencies." Definition from http://en.wikipedia. org/wiki/Social_Protection.

- Sustainable development: Development that "meets the needs of the present without compromising the ability of future generations to meet their own needs." Definition from the Report of the World Commission on Environment and Development (Brundtland Report 1987). Overall, sustainable development underlines the principle that the three pillars of sustainability should be integrated within decision-making and implementation.

- Three pillars of sustainability: Economic development, social development and environmental protection.

- Tripartism: Co-operation between governments, trade unions and employers (or their organizations). Within the International Labour Organization (ILO), tripartism involves social dialogue or "all types of negotiation, consultation, or exchange of information between, or among, representatives of governments, employers and workers, on the systems of commitment relating to social policy". From www.ilo.org/dyn/declaris/ DECLARATIONWEB.

- Utility green purchasing: Where utility green purchasing is in effect, customers' electricity demand may be supplied by renewable energy feeding into the power grid. See energy certificates, green power purchasing/green marketing.

- Workers and trade unions: One of the nine major civil society groups defined in Agenda 21, Section III. Chapter 29 of Agenda 21 specifies that "workers and trade unions should play an active role in the sustainable development activities of international and regional organizations, particularly within the United Nations system." A common definition of a trade union is "an organization of workers that promotes and protects the interests of its members in issues such as wages and working conditions, especially through negotiations with employers" (www.fieldsofhope.org/resources/glossary. asp).

- Working poor: Those whose work generates an income level below official poverty rates. "Today there are 550 million people who work, but still live on less than US$ 1 a day. These 'working poor' represent 20 per cent of total world employment. In spite of the record levels of global unemployment, the reality for most of the world's poor is that they must work – often for long hours, in poor working conditions and without basic rights and representation – at work that is not productive enough to enable them to lift themselves and their families out of poverty. While it is clearly the case that employment is central to poverty reduction, it is 'decent and productive' employment that matters, not employment alone." From the ILO's Employment Strategy web page (www.ilo.org/public/english/employment/strat/wer2004.htm). Also see decent work.

Selected Websites

African Growth and Opportunity Act (AGOA) (www.agoa.gov).

American Conference of Governmental Industrial Hygienists (ACGIH) (www.acgih.org)

Apollo Alliance (www.apolloalliance.org)

Asian Development Bank (ADB) Water for All web page (www.adb.org/Water)

Asian Workers Occupational Health, Safety and Environment Institute (www.ohseinstitute.org).

Basel Convention on the Control of Transboundary Movements of Hazardous Wastes and their Disposal (www.basel.int)

Confederación General del Trabajo (CGTRA) General Confederation of Labour, Argentina) (www.cgtra.org.ar)

Confederation of Independent Trade Unions of Bulgaria (KNSB/CITUB) (www.knsb-bg.or)

Deutscher Gewerkschaftsbund (DGB) (www.dgb.de)

Energy Information Agency, United States (EIA) (www.eia.doe.gov/environment.html).

Ethical Trading Initiative (www.ethicaltrade.org)

European Respiratory Society (ERS) (www.ersnet.org/ers)

European Trade Union Confederation (ETUC) (www.etuc.org)

European Union REACH Campaign (http://ec.europa.eu/environment/chemicals/reach/reach_intro.htm)

Federation of Free Trade Unions of Russia (FNPR) (www.fnpr.org.ru)

Freshwater Action Network (FAN) (www.freshwateraction.net/web/w/www_60_en.aspx)

German Technical Cooperation Agency (www.gzt.de)

Global e-Sustainability Initiative (www.gesi.org)

Global Footprint Network (www.footprintnetwork.org)

Global Labour University (GLU) (www.global-labour-university.org).

Global Reporting Initiative (www.globalreporting.org)

Global Union Research Network (GURN) (www.gurn.info).

Global Unions (www.global-unions.org)

Gold Mining Cyanide Code (www.cyanidecode.org)

Intergovernmental Panel on Climate Change (IPCC) (www.ipcc.ch)

International Chemical Safety Cards (ICSCs) (www.ilo.org/public/english/protection/safework/cis/products/icsc)

International Confederation of Free Trade Unions (ICFTU) (www.icftu.org)

International Decade of Education for Sustainable Development (http://portal.unesco.org/education/en/ev.php-URL_ID=27234&URL_DO=DO_TOPIC&URL_SECTION=201.html)

International Labour Foundation for Sustainable Development (Sustainlabour) (www.sustainlabour.org)

International Labour Organization (ILO) (www.ilo.org)

International Labour organization (ILO) Better Factories Cambodia Initiative (www.betterfactories.org/ILO/default.aspx?z=1&c=1)

International Labour organization (ILO) Better health and safety for suppliers (http://www.ilo.org/public/english/protection/safework/li_suppliers/).

International Labour Organization (ILO) Bureau for Workers' Activities (ACTRAV) (www.ilo.org/public/english/dialogue/actrav)

International Labour organization (ILO) International Training Centre (Turin, Italy) (www.itcilo.it/actrav)

International Labour organization (ILO) Locally Developed Training Materials (www.ilo.org/public/english/dialogue/actrav/enviro/trainmat/localtmc.htm)

International Monetary Fund (www.imf.org)

International Organization for Standardization (ISO) (www.iso.org)

International Organization of Employers (IOE) (www.ioe-emp.org)

International Textile, Garment and Leather Workers' Federation (ITGLWF) (www.itglwf.org)

International Trade Union Confederation (ITUC) (www.ituc-csi.org)

Investors and Environmentalists for Sustainable Prosperity (CERES) (www.ceres.org)

Johannesburg Plan of Implementation (www.un.org/esa/sustdev/documents/WSSD_POI_PD/English/POIToc.htm)

Kyoto Protocol to the UN Framework Convention on Climate Change (http://unfccc.int/kyoto_protocol/items/2830.php)

Marrakech Co-operation Dialogue with Development Agencies (www.unep.fr/pc/sustain/10year/CooCo-operation%20Dialogue.htm)

Marrakech Process meeting reports (www.unep.fr/pc/sustain/10year/home.htm)

Marrakech Task Forces (www.unep.fr/pc/sustain/10year/taskforce.htm)

Millennium Development Goals (www.un.org/millenniumgoals)

Millennium Ecosystem Assessment (MA) (www.maweb.org)

New Partnership for Africa's Development (NEPAD) (www.nepad.org)

Nigeria Labour Congress (NLC) (www.nlcng.org).

Norwegian Confederation of Trade Unions (www.lo.no).

Office of the UN High Commissioner for Human Rights (OHCRH) (www.ohcrh.ch)

Organisation for Economic Cooperation and Development (OECD) (www.oecd.org)

Organisation for Economic Co-operation and Development (www.oecd.org)

REN21 Renewable Energy Policy Network (www.ren21.net)

Tour Operators Initiative (www.toinitiative.org)

Trade Union Advisory Committee (TUAC) to the OECD (www.tuac.org)

Trade Union Sustainable Development Advisory Committee (http://www.defra.gov.uk/environment/tusdac/)

Trade Union Sustainable Development Unit (Trade Union Country-by-Country Profiles) (www.tradeunionsdunit.org/profiles)

Trades Unions Congress (TUC) of the United Kingdom (learning initiatives web page) (www.unionlearn.org.uk)

United Nations Environment Programme (UNEP) Chemicals (www.chem.unep.ch).

United Nations Environment Programme (UNEP) Division of Technology, Industry and Economics (www.uneptie.org)

United Nations Environment Programme (UNEP) Energy Branch - Mobility Forum (www.uneptie.org/energy/act/tp/amf/index.htm)

United Nations Environment Programme (UNEP) Finance Initiative (www.unepfi.org)

United Nations Environment Programme (UNEP) Global Civil Society Forum (www.unep.org/civil_society/GCSF/)

United Nations Environment Programme (UNEP) Global Environment outlook 3 (GEO -3) Data Compendium (http://geocompendium.grid.unep.ch)

United Nations Environment Programme (UNEP) Global Environment Outlook 3 (GEO-3) (www.unep.org/geo/geo3)

United Nations Environment Programme (UNEP) Labour and the Environment Initiative (www.unep.org/labour_environment/)

United Nations Environment Programme (UNEP) Major Groups and Stakeholders Branch (www.unep.org/civil_society/)

United Nations Environment Programme (UNEP) Production and Consumption Branch - Advertising and Communication Forum (www.uneptie.org/pc/sustain/advertising/advertising.htm).

United Nations Environment Programme (UNEP) Production and Consumption Branch - Sustainable Buildings and Construction Initiative (www.uneptie.org/pc/pc/SBCI/UNEP%20Sustainable%20Building%20and%20Construction%20Initiative.pdf)

United Nations Environment Programme (UNEP) WAVE (Women As the Voice for the Environment) (www.unep.org/civil_society/WAVE/)

Union of Concerned Scientists (www.ucsusa.org)

United Nations (www.un.org)

United Nations Commission on Sustainable Development (UNCSD) (www.un.org/esa/sustdev/csd/policy.htm)

United Nations Development Programme (UNDP) (www.undp.org)

United Nations Division for Sustainable Development (www.un.org/esa/sustdev)

United Nations Division for Sustainable Development (www.un.org/esa/sustdev)

United Nations Division for the Advancement of Women (www.un.org/womenwatch/daw/daw/index.html)

United Nations Division of Economic and Social Affairs (www.un.org/esa/desa/)

United Nations Educational. Scientific and Cultural Organization (UNESCO) (www.unesco.org)

United Nations Framework Convention on Climate Change (http://unfccc.int)

United Nations Global Compact (www.unglobalcompact.org).

United Nations Guidelines for Consumer Protection (www.un.org/esa/sustdev/sdissues/consumption/cpp1225.htm)

United Nations Human Settlements Programme (UN HABITAT) Water and Sanitation (www.unhabitat.org/categories.asp?catid=270)

United Nations Industrial Development Organization (UNIDO) (www.unido.org)

United Nations Office on Drugs and Crime (UNODC) (www.unodc.com)

United Nations Statistics Division (http://unstats.un.org)

United Nations Sustainable Development Case Studies (http://webapps01.un.org/dsd/caseStudy/public/Welcome.do)

United Nations World Tourism Organization (UNWTO) (www.world-tourism.org)

United States Department of Labor, Bureau of Labor Statistics (www.bls.gov)

United States National Oceanic and Atmospheric Administration (NOAA) (www.noaa.gov)

Varda Group (www.vardagroup.org)

Wine Industry Ethical Trade Association (South Africa) (www.wieta.org.za).

World Bank Water Supply and Sanitation (http://web.worldbank.org/WBSITE/EXTERNAL/ TOPICS/EXTWSS/0,,menuPK:337308~pagePK:149018~piPK:149093~theSitePK:337302,00. html)

World Business Council for Sustainable Development (WBCSD) (www.wbcsd.ch)

World Confederation of Labour (WCL) (www.cmt-wcl.org)

World Health Organization (WHO) International Agency for Research on Cancer (IARS) (www.iarc.fr)

World Health Organization (WHO) Occupational Health web page (www.who.int/topics/ occupational_health/en)

World Health Organization (WHO) (www.who.org)

World Health Organization (WHO) Children's Environmental Health web page (www.who. int/ceh/en)

World Health Organization (WHO) Drinking Water (www.who.int/topics/drinking_water/en/)

World Health Organization (WHO) Quantifying Environmental Health Impacts web page (www.who.int/quantifying_ehimpacts/en)

World Health Organization (WHO) Water, Sanitation and Health web page (www.who.int/ water_sanitation_health/en/)

World Meteorological Organization (WMO) (www.wmo.ch)

Worldwatch Institute (www.worldwatch.org)

Authors

- Mr. **Gerd Albracht** is Senior Specialist in Occupational Safety and Health, and Coordinator for the Development of Inspection Systems, at the International Labour Office. Starting as a chemical engineer, he attended the Technical University of Berlin and graduated with an MSc in chemistry. Four more years of scientific work were followed by employment at the German Chemistry, Paper and Ceramics Union (IGCPK) in Hannover, Germany. He was Director of its Environmental Protection Unit from 1977-85 and was appointed Executive Secretary. In 1985 Mr. Albracht became Ministerial Department Director and head of Environmental Policy and Waste Management in the Ministry of Labour and the Environment, and until 2002 was director for Health and Safety in the Labour Ministry of the State of Hesse, Germany. In 2002 he went to work at the International Labour Organization (ILO)/Safework. He served for ten years as President of the International Association of Labour Inspectors (IALI) and has been a member of the EU Senior Labour Inspectors Committee.

- Mr **Nilvo Luis Alves Da Silva** joined UNEP's Major Groups and Stakeholders Branch in 2005. A chemical engineer with Master's degrees in ecology and environmental planning and management, Mr. Silva worked for more than 15 years in environmental planning and management at the municipal, state and federal levels in Brazil. He has extensive experience with the intersection of social and environmental matters, and with multi-stakeholder policy-making forums. He was CEO of the Environmental Agency of the State of Rio Grande do Sul, Brazil, and Deputy-President of the Brazilian Institute for the Environment and Natural Renewable Resources.

- Ms. **Sophie De Coninck** works for the Major Groups and Stakeholders' Branch of the Division of Regional Cooperation at UNEP. She holds Master's degrees in engineering and management, and in environmental science and management. Prior to her work at UNEP, she was involved in industry and in environmental consulting. Specialized in sustainable consumption and behaviour, she also worked as a researcher and published a series of articles on policy development in the fields of sustainable mobility, energy consumption, land use planning, climate change mitigation, and housing and poverty.

- Dr. **Igor Fedotov** is Senior Specialist on Occupational Health in the International Programme on Safety and Health at Work and the Environment at ILO headquarters in Geneva, Switzerland. A medical doctor, he also holds a PhD in occupational medicine. During his career at ILO, which started in 1987, he has been the ILO Regional Advisor for South Asia. His main areas of activity include development of occupational health practice, occupational health services, prevention of occupational respiratory diseases, elimination of silica- and asbestos-related diseases, promotion of workplace health, and promotion of international co-operation in occupational health. He is the author of numerous publications on occupational health.

- Ms. **Hilary French** is a Special Advisor to UNEP's Division of Regional Cooperation. In this capacity, she works closely with the division's Major Groups and Stakeholder's Branch and with UNEP's Regional Office for North America. Ms. French also works for Worldwatch Institute in Washington, DC, where she is currently Senior Advisor for Programs. She has published widely on global environmental and sustainable development issues. She is the author of *Vanishing Borders Protecting the Planet in the Age of Globalization* and the co-author of 12 of Worldwatch Institute's annual *State of the World* reports.

- Dr **Ivan Dimov Ivanov** is a scientist specializing in occupational health at the Department for Public Health and Environment, WHO headquarters (Geneva), where he deals with the development and implementation of global policies for the protection and promotion of workers' health. Dr Ivanov is a medical doctor with an MPH in occupational health from his native country, Bulgaria, and a PhD in the sociology of health and environment from Michigan State University (USA). Before coming to WHO headquarters, he worked in the WHO Regional Office for Europe in Copenhagen and the Bulgarian Ministry of Health. Dr Ivanov is an Adjunct Assistant Professor at the Institute of International Health at Michigan State University.

- Dr. **Olfa Khazri** was born in Tunisia in 1970. She received her Master's degree in Tunisia and her PhD from the University of Quebec at Montreal (UQAM). She has taught at the Business School of Tunis (Ecole Supérieure de Commerce de Tunis), the University of Sherbrooke (Canada) and UQAM in Quebec. She is an assistant researcher for the project of the forest management under zoning programmes (TRIAD) in GREFi (Groupe de Recherche en Ecologie Forestière interuniversitaire, Canada). Dr. Khazri worked at ILO in 2006. Her principal research interests are microeconomics, natural resources, environmental economics and political economy

- Ms. **Fatou Ndoye** works for the Major Groups and Stakeholders' Branch of the Division of Regional Cooperation at UNEP. She holds a Master's degree in languages (English and Spanish) and a certificate in Environment and Development from LEAD International. She has previously worked for and headed an international NGO, where she collaborated on the elaboration of the Global Environment Outlook report series and its Africa Environment Outlook. She has expertise in information and communication, networking with international organizations, international and regional NGOs, project development and execution, and policy documents analysis and strategies development in relation to sustainable development.

- Mr. **Joaquín Nieto** has always been engaged in social causes. Since 1991 he has assumed environmental responsibility in the main Spanish Union Confederation (Comisiones Obreras). He was the co-founder and President of the International Labour Foundation for Sustainable Development (Sustainlabour), established by trade unionists from Africa, Asia, America and Europe to promote international agreements on sustainable development and environment at the workplace. He was among the representatives of workers at the Johannesburg Summit, and at the CSD and UNFCCC-COPs since 2002. He is a member of the Environmental Advisory Council of the Spanish Environmental Ministry; Vice-President of the Occupational Health and Safety National Commission; and a member of the National Council on Climate. Mr. Nieto is also a member of National Council on Forests; a former member of European Consultative Forum on the Environment and Sustainable Development (1996-2001); and founder and President of ISTAS (the Trade Union Institute for Work, Environment and Health).

- Ms. **Lene Olsen** works in the International Labour Organization's Bureau for Workers' Activities (ILO/ACTRAV). She is in charge of environmentally sustainable development issues, in addition to being involved in the Global Union Research Network (GURN) and the Global Labour University (GLU). She also covers issues related to information technology. For two years Ms. Olsen worked on the ILO/ACTRAV environment project dealing with workers' education and environment, and on two child labour projects aimed at developing national and international trade union strategies to combat child labour, as well as actions against child labour through education and training. Before joining the ILO in 1999, she worked for six years for the Brussels office of the Norwegian Confederation of Trade Unions.

- **Mr. Peter Poschen** is Senior Policy Specialist in the Policy Integration Department of the ILO. He has a long-standing interest, and some 25 years of professional experience, with the social dimensions of sustainable development. Originally trained as a forester, he studied land-use systems in Costa Rica and Ethiopia for his Master's and PhD degrees. These experiences convinced him that people are both the problem and the solution for sustainable development. His current work focuses on the links between decent work and sustainable development, particularly the social and labour impacts of climate change.

- Mr. **Lucien Royer** is the trade union international coordinator for occupational health, environment, sustainable development and HIV/AIDS. He has a long history of engagement and publications, dealing with environmental protection through the world of work, workplaces and workers. He coordinates the trade union activity in UN and other institutions that are connected to his field of work.

- Mr. **Tony Musu** graduated from the University of Brussels with a degree in chemical engineering. He holds a PhD in science from the Pasteur Institute in Paris. After obtaining his PhD, he spent five years in the advanced research centre at L'Oréal, working on the safety assessment of chemicals. Since September 2003 he has been at the Research Institute of the European Trade Union Confederation (ETUI-REHS/ETUC). On behalf of ETUC, he participates in various REACH-related EU working groups. He is also a member of the Ad Hoc Working Group on Chemicals within the Luxembourg Advisory Committee on Health and Safety at Work.

- Ms. **Shizue Tomoda** joined the ILO in 1982, after teaching for five years in Japan. She has worked in different units at the Geneva headquarters, as well as in ILO field offices in Indonesia and Sri Lanka. During her career at the ILO, she has dealt with gender and labour force participation issues, mostly in developing countries, and employment and various labour issues in specific economic sectors such as tourism and food and drink manufacturing. Since 2001 she has been the Senior Sectoral Specialist responsible for public services and the utilities sector in the Sectoral Activities Department.

- Mr. **Cornis van der Lugt,** a South African by birth, is based in Paris at UNEP's Division of Technology, Industry and Economics (DTIE), where he is responsible for corporate responsibility (CESR), the Global Compact (GC) of the UN Secretary-General and the Global Reporting Initiative (GRI). In recent years he has represented UNEP and the GC at various international conferences and in GRI expert working groups. He is also the GC nominated expert in the ISO process to develop a standard on social responsibility, building on his close involvement in promoting UNEP-business partnership and accountability. He has carried out long-standing research in the field of international political economy, focusing on the environment and the roles of business and industry. He received his PhD in international relations from the University of Stellenbosch in 1998. His doctoral studies involved research at the Albert-Ludwigs-Universität Freiburg (Germany; DAAD stipendium) and the Rijksuniversiteit Leiden (Netherlands; Stichting Studienfonds scholarship), following which he gained experience as multilateral diplomat in international negotiations under the UN agreements on climate change and ozone depletion.

- Ms. **Monika G. Wehrle-MacDevette's** experience in research, and the application of physiology and developmental genetics of living systems in response to stressful environments, provides the basis for her interest in the impacts of environmental change on human health and well-being. She worked in South Africa from 1992-2001 on environmental technologies for small business development, and in Kuwait with an international team evaluating research needs related to the environmental effects of war on human health and groundwater contamination. She joined the regional co-ordination group of UNEP in 2003 and has been involved in the development of a revised Environment and Health strategy for UNEP.

- Ms. **Adriana Zacarias Farah** is Project Co-ordinator at UNEP's Division of Technology, Industry and Economics (DTIE), based in Paris. She co-ordinates development of the 10-Year Framework of Programmes on Sustainable Consumption and Production at the global and regional level, including Africa, Asia, Europe, Latin America and North America. She also carries out projects on implementation of the UN Guidelines on Consumer Protection and works on linkages between poverty reduction and sustainable consumption and production. Before joining UNEP, she was a consultant in the Environment Directorate of the Organisation for Economic Co-operation and Development, where she was responsible for the publication of *Towards Sustainable Household Consumption* (OECD, 2002). Ms. Zacarias Farah has a Master's degree in environment and development from Cambridge University, UK, and a degree in political science from the Instituto Tecnológico Autónomo de Mexico (ITAM).

- Ms. **Daniela Zampini** works in the ILO's Multinational Enterprises Programme, where she is an expert on the Global Compact and on corporate social responsibility (CSR). She co-ordinates projects and research work on piloting CSR through globally agreed guidelines. Between 1997 and 2004, she held field assignments as researcher and project manager for various NGOs and UN organizations, including UNESCO and UNDP, travelling extensively in sub-Saharan Africa and the Middle East. Her activities have mostly concentrated in the areas of corporate responsibility, trade, private sector development and public-private partnership. Ms. Zampini holds degrees in economics and social sciences and in economic development from Bocconi University in Italy and from the University of Glasgow in Scotland (UK).

EP 02/07/#06-54675